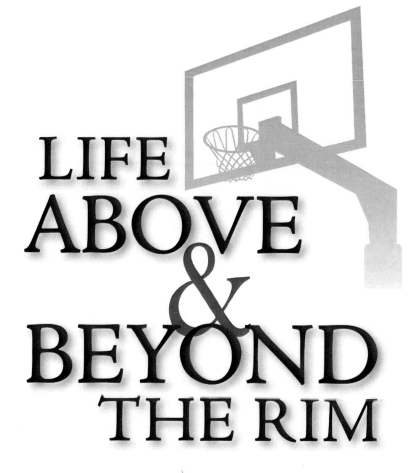

# LIFE ABOVE & BEYOND THE RIM

10 principles to break through barriers
and elevate success in your life

## JOE COURTNEY

iUniverse LLC
Bloomington

# LIFE ABOVE & BEYOND THE RIM

*iUniverse books may be ordered through booksellers or by contacting:*

*iUniverse*
*1663 Liberty Drive*
*Bloomington, IN 47403*
*www.iuniverse.com*
*1-800-Authors (1-800-288-4677)*

*ISBN: 978-1-4917-3562-6 (sc)*
*ISBN: 978-1-4917-3561-9 (e)*

*Library of Congress Control Number: 2014910168*

*Printed in the United States of America.*

*iUniverse rev. date: 6/19/2014*

**I**WOULD LIKE TO THANK GOD FOR MY JOURNEY IN LIFE AND THE EXPERIENCES that led me to write this book. *Life above and beyond the Rim* is dedicated to all the people who strive to break through their barriers to have ultimate success in life. To those people who have supported my endeavors to give something of value to every individual who comes in contact with me. All the people who have allowed me to coach them and lead them, trusting and allowing me to go inside their souls to help repair them from the inside out. To the owners and management of the companies, groups, and institutions that gave me the privilege to speak and impact their people. To the people who sat in those seats listening and opening up their minds for me to deliver my concept. To my friends, family, siblings, business partners, and peers for the experiences and for being true to who they are, because what I have learned through our journeys has taught me some of life's most precious and valuable lessons.

This book is dedicated to my son, Chase Courtney, who makes me feel like the most important person on earth—by looking up to me, yearning for my attention, and loving me unconditionally. You, Chase, are the most important part of my legacy and the people you and I touch together. My wish is that you use this book as a tool to achieve an empowered, successful, fulfilled, and complete life. You have taught me more about the importance of the value of life and why we need to empower people than anything I've ever done.

Everyone has had a dream at some point and time and was born with the ability to be great at something in his or her life. Through our own personal journeys, we have been beaten, battered, and bruised from the challenges life has thrown at us until we have forgotten that we are capable and have even lost our ability to dream again. Deep inside of us, we unconsciously know that there is greatness from within that is waiting to be unleashed. This book is dedicated to unlocking that greatness so that you can soar above and beyond and have the success in life you deserve!

# CONTENTS

# PREFACE

**H**ELLO! MY NAME IS JOE COURTNEY. MY LIFE HAS BEEN A COLLECTION OF amazing experiences, some of which I will share with you in this book. I thank you for sharing your personal space with me and using this book as a tool to assist you in your journey to ultimate success. You might have seen my life as a NBA basketball player; you might have walked through one of the homes I designed and built, or maybe you attended one of my speaking events or my *Above the Rim* coaching seminars.

I'm an entrepreneur who has been fortunate enough to have achieved success in numerous endeavors. Like everyone who strives for success, I have had challenges that go with such a journey. When I went through challenges, I used to ask God, "Why me?" Sound familiar? Well, I recently found out "why me." Over time, I realized I have a certain perspective that has been the X factor for me as I've gone through my life; I'm six feet nine, tall enough to see a lot from up here. This perspective has assisted me in my journey to reach success. People who have been fortunate enough to achieve success have not completed their missions until they have shared their experiences with others to pave the way and simplify the process for others to also achieve success. This creates a butterfly effect—success multiplies each generation it touches.

That's why I'm writing this book. For years, I thought I was alone in the positive and negative experiences I've been through. But over time, as I moved from one field of work to the next, I realized there was a common denominator not only within me but also within all people; it just takes on a different look, a different face. As I kept seeing this, I realized I needed to share what I had to say with the world because I feel it would be of value to others in unlocking their hidden gems.

I was told once that when you compile your experiences, what you learn from your successes as well as your failures constitutes your life's work.

My true purpose for writing this book is to document the ten key principles I have used to reach successes in my life and also to compare, reference, and validate them with the works of some of the great leaders of our time. I've played on a world-championship team and was coached by the best coaches in the world, I've trained with the some of the best physical and mental trainers in the world, and I've run my own companies and have been mentored by the best in the industry.

I've taken key elements from all my experiences to formulate the information I'm passing on to you. Through speaking and coaching, I've tested these principles and found they are truly effective in helping people reach success on all levels in multiple types of industries. I present to you my life's work, *Life above and beyond the Rim.* Enjoy, and God bless!

# ACKNOWLEDGMENTS

I express my gratitude to the people who inspired me through my journey and the amazing people who were put in my path to create the experiences I've gone through in the evolution of this book.

As an artist, I created work people have shown their appreciation for, and I've been humbled to be appreciated for my work. But I acknowledge that like the homes I've built and my NBA highlights, this book was inspired by my past experiences and other books I've read, leaders I've been led by, speakers I've heard, and lessons I've learned. The following are some of those people.

## Michael Jordan

Thank you for making the time I spent with the three-peat Chicago Bulls one of the best experiences of my life. Thank you for the private life lessons you've given me on and off the court and for making sure I was taken care of. You showed me what work really was and what true leaders do. Thanks for believing in me and telling me that I belonged in the NBA and that I was put on earth to do something great.

## Tim Grover

You showed me my limits in life and performance were only in my mind. You treated me like a professional athlete, and then you made me one, and I was in the best physical and mental shape in my life. You are the best in the world at what you do. Thank you.

## Phil Jackson

You taught me the power of leading without words and that silence can be strength. You taught me the importance of a system and creating a winning culture of accountability. You made me a champion. Thank you.

## Charles Barkley

What can I say, "Chuckster"? Thank you for showing me how to work hard and play hard. You took care of me when I was supposed to be taking care of you, and you told me to keep my money until I was rich when I offered to pay. I had the most fun in my life while playing with you.

## Jerry Colangelo

You saw the fire in my eyes, took a chance on me, and gave me the opportunity to prove myself at a pivotal time in my life. You are a class act. I met my beautiful wife, had my son, and moved my family to Arizona because you took that chance on me. You're the best owner the NBA has ever seen. Thank you.

## Paul Westphal

Thank you for playing me to my strengths. I couldn't dribble with my left hand when I came to the NBA, but you ignored that and focused on what I could do. You empowered me. Thank you.

## Lionel Hollins

You fought hard for Coach Westphal and Jerry Colangelo to give me a shot. I wouldn't have played for the Suns if you hadn't believed in me first at the Utah Summer League. Thank you for recognizing my potential and standing up for me.

## Eddie Johnson

Thank you for being there with advice throughout my career. You are a valuable asset and friend.

## John Lang

You took an interest in me and reminded me to keep my head high no matter what was going on in my life. You took time and moved meetings to listen to me and provided a confidential, safe place for me to vent my ideas. You are an example of someone taking 100 percent responsibility for his life. Thank you.

## Mack Newton

You are a once-in-a-lifetime leader. They truly broke the mold after you. You lead by example and are the purest source of dedication I've seen since Jordan. Thank you for giving me the gift of an extended life. You taught me the basics of nutrition and how to stay in shape in a six-by-three-foot space anywhere in the world. You saved my life. Thank you!

## Blair Singer

Thank you for the straight advice when I was creating my program. You were gracious and gave me support to go for it. You are an example of practicing what you preach.

## Mark Cuban

Thank you for being a model example of an NBA owner and providing a true platform for athletes to prosper on and off the court. You are an example of empowering others. Thank you

## My Wife, Lee Courtney

To my beautiful wife: you have been an amazing rock for more than twenty years. You gave me the most amazing son a man could want. Thank you for being the best mother to Chase. For all the late nights I was working and you kept him occupied even though you were tired also, I thank you.

## My Mother

Thank you for loving me unconditionally, feeding me with positivity, and visualizing my future with me. You encouraged me by saying I could become anything I wanted. Thank you for pointing out I should try basketball.

## Dr. Fredrick Price

You provided a Christian foundation and provided stability for my family. You were a staple when I was growing up and made the Word of God simple, precise, and easy to understand. Thank you.

## Joel Osteen

You have provided a staple for my family especially as my son grows older. You deliver the message of empowerment in a way that our future generation can understand therefore going beyond the rim. Thank you.

## Rick Whitlow

You saw greatness in me and used your platform as a sports reporter to give me the press I needed to go from high school to college. You followed my journey through life and celebrated my successes. Thank you.

## Kim West

Thank you for being the best in consulting with me about writing this book. You were patient, knowledgeable, and honest. You called me twenty-six times after my original inquiry and finally convinced me that my message was worth hearing. You returned my calls and answered my questions; you're a true example that persistence pays off. You're the best.

Our lives are formed by the experiences we have and the choices we make. The people who plant the seeds of support, love, and positivity in life contribute to forming who we become. All these people and many more friends, family, and associates have exemplified through our interactions parts of the message you're about to read in this book. I acknowledge you and thank you.

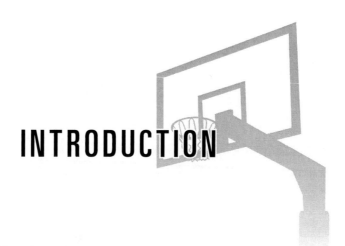

# INTRODUCTION

IT'S JANUARY 15, 1993. I'M SITTING ON THE BENCH IN ONE OF THE MOST
amazing and memorable places to play, the Chicago Bulls arena. For
years I'd watched arguably the greatest basketball player in the world
make history here. Nervous but anxious to prove I belong, I wait for the
call. I've had just a taste of the NBA floor once previously; I want the
right opportunity to make a name for myself. The game's in play, and
on the court are my teammates Michael Jordan, BJ Armstrong, Scottie
Pippen, Horace Grant, and Bill Cartwright.

I try to stay focused and ready just in case my name is called. I
was absorbed by the action I was viewing, just like all the fans in the
stadium. I had watched and admired these players in the years leading
up to my entry into the NBA. A thunderous call, "Courtney!" comes
from legendary coach Phil Jackson. This is it. It's finally my turn to show
what I can do. I jump to my feet and run to the huddle, looking Jackson
in the eyes to make sure I'd heard him right.

Jackson has his clipboard and marker ready to draw the play in the
huddle. I look at the players and take in the moment—Scott Williams,
BJ Armstrong, Trent Tucker, Michael Jordan, and me. I can feel my
heart beat. I tell myself, *Just stay calm. Take your time and run up and
down the court a few times to get loose and warm up.* I was listening and
watching the play being drawn up. *Okay, I think I'm ready.* Phil says,
"Courtney, you throw the ball in to Michael, cut back door. Michael,
pass the ball to Courtney. Courtney, finish the play. Break!" My heart

is in my throat now. Did I hear that right? Michael Jordan is passing me the ball to finish the play? Wow. Be careful for what you pray for, but I'm getting my chance! It dawns on me that my plans to warm up a bit is out the window. It's game time!

The whistle blows. The play starts. I pass the ball to Michael, and like clockwork, my defender leaves me to double-team Jordan, leaving me wide open. I cut back door. Jordan passes me the ball. I take a giant leap but realize I'm a ways from the rim. It's too late. I'm airborne. One way or another, destiny is about to happen. The center runs over to block my shot. Full of adrenaline, I soar. I keep climbing higher and higher. Up and over! I dunk the ball and yell with excitement. I land and look around. Michael's cheering me on, saying, "Way to go, Joe!" I know I've arrived; I belong in the NBA.

I was fortunate enough to play professional basketball for ten years. I had the unique opportunity to play for several teams in the NBA, including the three-peat championship Chicago Bulls, Golden State Warriors, Phoenix Suns, Milwaukee Bucks, Cleveland Cavaliers, Philadelphia 76ers, and the San Antonio Spurs.

When my amazing son, Chase Courtney, was born in 2000, my life and priorities changed forever. I retired early from basketball in 2001 at age thirty-one. In my journey to success in pro sports and later in the business world, I came to realize that certain experiences, thoughts, and decisions had helped me become successful. Some may think it was a sad moment for me when I retired from such a fun, exciting, and great sport. Though I was somewhat saddened to close that chapter of my life, I was equally excited to start the next.

I had majored in architecture in college, and deep down, I couldn't wait to pursue my dream of designing and building luxury homes. I brought the tools that had helped me attain success in sports to the business world. I started my companies and began experiencing success in a very short time.

As many recall, the years 2001 to 2008 were the "roaring 2000s." I was having a blast following my passion and making great money at the same time. But for some reason, I had the gut feeling that my soaring high in the business world wasn't going to last. In August 2007, signs of things to come were starting to bleed through. Banks started cutting credit lines for builders. Many of my colleagues who needed credit started panicking and even going out of business. My company started to get concerned, but we were fortunate enough to have liquidity. Nonetheless, we braced ourselves for what we know now was the "Great Recession." One after another, banks began to implode. Our bank went under, and millions of our liquidity went with it.

After the heavy economic waves of 2008 and 2009 came crashing down, my family as well as so many others in the world was faced with having to start over. I learned I had to dig deeper than I had ever done before and get in touch with my core principles that had helped me achieve in the first place. But this time it was different. I experienced not only financial damage but also a huge psychological setback that came with such a traumatic event. Everybody I knew was going through the same thing; I was on a level playing field. I was looking at my past years of hard work that seemed to have just gone down the drain. Like everyone else, I felt crushed. I was at a loss. I felt empty. Even though I had plenty of reasons to feel down (and I went through a period of doing just that), I knew in my heart it was time to get my life back. I started the process of my comeback in business. I began my search by looking back on my life, reflecting on and understanding the principles of success that had served me then. I tried to figure out what had set me apart.

I'd been blessed with success in my life, but I certainly hadn't been born into it. I ended up playing basketball on a championship team, but I hadn't started life that strong. How had I, a kid who hadn't even picked up a basketball until the end of freshman year in high school, (that's the 10th grade where I'm from), actually made it to the NBA? Even more important, how did that kid go on to pivot from the lofty heights of professional sports to success in real estate and the design-and-build industry?

When I started my building company, I had to focus on the most important elements to become successful in the industry, so I needed to concentrate only on the matters that would allow me to fulfill my dream and not get distracted by the minutiae. I was result-oriented; I studied the correct way to build my houses, and I mentored with people at the top of their game in the business. Most important, I stayed on task with my passion and always kept the desired outcome in mind. As a result, I had accomplished in five years what it took most others fifteen and even twenty years to accomplish. My work was featured in numerous publications, including *Architectural Digest*. I crafted beautiful properties that my wife and I sold for millions. It was an amazing experience.

As I reflect on my journey, I realize everyone desires success even though success means different things to different people. Sure, success to some means making millions, but to others, it means carving out comfortable lifestyles that allow them to enjoy time with friends and family. In spite of the wide range of definitions that success can have, some people reach their desired success and some don't. That's what intrigued me. I wanted to figure out what made some people successful but others less than successful. I've come up with ten keys to success that make all the difference.

The way I see it, we all have a rim in life (with apologies to any nonbasketball-loving readers). A personal rim is a set of expectations, a silent, hidden line beyond which we struggle to succeed. This line is the result of an internal collection of experiences and circumstances— everything that makes an individual who he or she is. However, most people don't realize it's there let alone understand that their choices, belief systems, environments, and other personal influences are responsible for its placement.

Self-awareness of your rim is the central driver behind attaining the self-confidence you need to battle adversity, especially if you fail at first. Self-awareness will equip you to get up and try again. You'll have the faith to push yourself toward your dreams while knowing your strengths as well as your weaknesses. After all, we're talking about your dreams here.

Success can be measured in many ways. The person content with a decent job and a happy family is considered successful if that is what that person dreams. Others will have dreams that will cause them to take on challenges they would otherwise not face. Some may have suppressed their dreams unknowingly and or created rims so low that they're assured success. It's an interesting conversation, but I know that people who are in touch with what they truly want in life and who experience true success learn to overcome their limitations and live their lives *above* their rims.

As you read through the ten keys to living life above the rim and reflect on your limitations, you'll do some serious introspection and discover where your personal rim is and what you can do to surpass it. We all set boundaries for ourselves, sometimes unconsciously, and some of us end up living within those self-imposed confines.

My goal with this book is to help you identify your boundaries and push them once you identify what they are, how they relate to your personal limitations, and how you can control and even conquer them. I want you to go beyond that by empowering others to do the same so not only you but all those in your life achieve success.

Think about it. You started out with dreams and aspirations to conquer the world one way or another. Are those dreams still thriving, or did you settle for less somewhere along the way? What about your neighborhood? Why do you live there? Was that a financial decision? If your dream is on the basic level of owning your own beautiful home and having a healthy, happy family and money in the bank, more power to you. Desiring to fulfill a dream will bring with it challenges, failures, successes, hardships, joys, and despair. If you stay at home watching TV and choose not to dream big, your life will have far fewer challenges than if you truly reach for the stars—whatever those stars may be.

Maybe you have a dream of becoming a classical, rock, or blues guitarist or a painter, actor, or athlete. Maybe you dream of climbing Mount Everest, canoeing the Amazon, or sailing the Atlantic. Maybe you want to own a business that reflects your passions and talents. Whatever it is, you have to be clear about the difference between your true dreams and those that have been whittled down by circumstance or your desire for immediate comfort.

For many people, everything comes back to where they work and how much they earn. While there's nothing wrong with that (responsible financial planning is paramount if you want to secure a comfortable retirement), it is often all too easy to overlook the fact that your entire life and all your relationships can end up revolving around that basic infrastructure. If the infrastructure that surrounds your whole life isn't built on the foundation of your real, deep dreams, if you're building a life by default based on a series of choices that seemed the easy way at the time, your real dreams will recede further from realization. One day you'll wake up and not even remember what those dreams were.

Dreams are unique to each individual, but they share common threads with others' dreams. If you dream or desire something, chances are someone has done it before and is living your dream right now. Because dreams vary from one individual to another, there are different catalysts for an individual's pursuit of his or her dream that come from two different sides of the coin. On one side it may be freedom of expression through individual passions such as art, music, writing, or poetry, while the other side could have purely financial considerations. The common thread could be the money that connects them.

While your dream should be based on your passion, financial freedom will often be the key to your ability to "buy" the time to express your passion, but don't let that be an excuse to settle or suppress your dream. In almost all cases, the dream ignites the vision, and that's followed by action and then money. You may suppress your dreams and settle for less, but that doesn't mean your passion will go away; it can haunt you and make you uncomfortable.

A big red flag that indicates you may have let your dreams slip away in favor of the relative comfort of mediocrity is when you catch yourself feeling uncomfortable around successful people. Perhaps when you were younger, you spied a really nice car and perhaps dreamed about owning one just like it someday. Then you got a little older, and your dreams drifted further away, and you stopped admiring nice cars. You started even ignoring them because they reminded you of what you hadn't achieved.

Of course, a car isn't everyone's symbol of success. Maybe for you it's seeing a happily married couple at a restaurant or watching someone performing the job you wish you had. If you feel uncomfortable or resentful around successful people, it's a sure sign your dreams are languishing somewhere in the dark recesses of a nearly forgotten corner of your mind.

But you do have a choice. You can live a better life, and you can rise above the rim. Those successful people didn't just wake up one morning under a big pile of money or to the sound of the phone ringing off the hook with job offers. They too had to work hard for their dreams. The first step toward realizing your own version of success is to learn the key principles that successful people live by. Luckily for you, they're all outlined in this book.

# CHAPTER

# DREAMS

## *I Believe I Can Fly*

*Every great dream begins with a dreamer. Always remember,*
*you have within you the strength, the patience, and the*
*passion to reach for the stars to change the world.*
—Harriet Tubman

CLOSE YOUR EYES AND IMAGINE DOING SOMETHING YOU'VE ALWAYS WANTED to do with no limits or expectations from others. You're enjoying the pure, raw emotion of fulfilling your passion. Picture your life at that moment; feel the sensation of happiness and peace that come with being fulfilled on your own terms. The pressures of life lift from your shoulders, and you feel almost weightless, hovering in the air. You start to fly, to soar in life. That's right—you start to dream.

All successful people begin with dreams. Sure, it seems obvious when you're reading this, but it's an absolutely crucial and all-too-often overlooked fact. Without a dream to work toward, nothing else matters. Take a look at any successful person and you'll find he or she had a dream.

What are your dreams today? What did they used to be? Are you living the life you dreamed of, or were your dreams shoved to the side to make room for a life born of the false comfort zone of easy decisions and no challenges? Before you can begin to understand yourself, where you are, and where you want to go, you need to pull your dreams out of the closet, dust them off, and put them out somewhere so you can see them every day. Without them, nothing will happen.

My dream to become and NBA player was actually uncovered one day when my friends and I were playing basketball. I dunked one ball, and that was followed by a sudden flurry of baskets I made. I didn't know where it had come from, but I suddenly realized I might have had the talent to play the game on a higher level. From that day on, I was obsessed. My dream was to become an NBA player.

That process started a short time earlier, when my father told me he wanted me to play sports. He was fond of football, but I never wanted to play that game. He was very aggressive when it came to delivering his sports message; let's just say his communication skills weren't the best. My mother pointed out that football wasn't the only sport; she suggested I try something else.

She and I were watching TV on the afternoon my basketball aspirations were born. She'd been channel surfing and landed on a basketball game. My mom and I got more and more excited as we watched a graceful Chicago Bulls player number 23 move up and down the court as if he had invented the sport. This guy was different. The more I watched him, the more I embraced the sport. From that game forward, my mom was adamant in her conviction that I too could become a professional basketball player even though I'd never dribbled a ball in my life. Though her conviction ignited my passion, the events that followed fueled my inner passion for the sport, and my dream was born.

The next day, I went to school with a wristband on my arm. As I walked past the gym, the basketball coach stopped me. "Son, what are you doing with that wristband on your arm?"

"I'm going to be a basketball player."

"You want to be a basketball player? The only way you can be a basketball player is if you join a team. Are you on a team?"

"Uh, no." I replied. It dawned on me he was right about me having to actually be on a team. He pointed out that he had known I wasn't on a team. He was the basketball coach after all. He asked me if I wanted to try out for basketball. I agreed to meet him after school.

Later that day, in the gym, he started bouncing the ball and said, "Okay, let's see what you've got. I'm going to send you a chest pass." As I reached my hands out to catch it, the ball went through my hands, hit me in the face, rolled down my chest and legs, and bounced off my feet. The ball just rolled away. I stood in stunned silence. The coach shook his head. "Alright, we've got our work cut out for us."

From that point on, I started to transform myself into a basketball player. It would have been far easier to just get discouraged and give up. No one would have blamed me for looking in a new direction. It was my first day touching a basketball, and it looked as though I had no skills. But my dream was big and intense. I wanted it. I could taste it. I knew I had to do whatever it took to make my dream reality.

I started working hard, doing whatever it took to make it onto the school team. My hard work paid off; I made the team. But even then, I never let up. I stayed after school to put in hours of extra practice—running drills; working on dribbling and ball handling skills; taking practice shots; and building strength, power, and agility in the workout room. I began to own my dream.

In junior year of high school, I broke a state record by blocking seventeen shots in one game. What an amazing achievement in one year! It was an early confirmation that by working hard and passionately believing in my dreams, I could achieve great things.

Even nature seemed to be in on it. Between my sophomore and senior year, I grew from six three to six eight and became one of the top high school basketball players in Mississippi. I was really starting to look the part of a basketball player. I still had some shortcomings and much work to do, but I was fitting the mold.

I got scholarships to play basketball in college, which proved to be a huge boost to my confidence. I attended the University of Southern Mississippi and Mississippi State. I majored in architecture and minored in advertising graphics. Though I had my sight on sports, I focused on my studies as additional insurance for my future. I loved the world of architecture as well as creating and designing, and I wanted to pursue this later in my life after sports.

As I continued to play ball and pursue my dream in college, I noticed everybody around me had dreams of some kind, some lower than others. Some teammates' dreams were just to get to college, some were to fulfill their parents' dreams of playing basketball in college, and a few of us had dreams deep in our hearts of going all the way to the NBA.

But I wasn't there at that point. I was playing college ball in a corner of southern Mississippi. No doubt I'd come a long way, but I couldn't let up. I kept doing the same thing that had brought me to where I was—working hard and staying connected to my dream.

When things didn't progress for me as quickly as they had in the beginning, I started to get a little discouraged. In my junior year, I watched the Chicago Bulls playing in the championships on TV. I remember how Michael Jordan stood there hugging the championship trophy and a basketball after the game. He was soaked in sweat, and tears were running down his face. He was hugging that ball as if it were the last one on earth.

I wanted that!

Just as he had helped spark my dreams in high school, Michael Jordan once again set fire to my passion and continued to be a symbol of my dreams. His success made me want to elevate myself. With renewed fervor, I began to work harder than ever and once again started to see results. I put in extra miles running at night to get in the best shape I could to beat the statistics that said I, a modestly good college player, would never make it to the NBA. I sweated my way up from the middle to becoming one of the best players on our college team.

My dream became reality when I went to the Chicago Bulls training camp and, while there, signed with that world champion team. I was standing on the same court as Michael Jordan did; my locker was next to his.

The whole thing really came full circle for me one day as Michael and I were in a limousine about to leave after a game. He was on his way to shoot a commercial and was still in uniform. A kid came running up to the limo and asked, "Mr. Jordan, Can I please have your wristband?" I watched Michael Jordan pull off his wristband and reach over me to hand it to the kid. Time stood still for me. I remembered the first day I stayed after school with the high school basketball coach, wearing my own wristband. I remembered how the inspiration carried me through my college slump. And here I was, living my dream.

CHAPTER ONE

## Principle 1: The Importance of Dreams

Successful people have something in common. If you follow their trail of success back in their past, you will find a dream. The principle of dreams is essential to unlocking the success in you. It allows you to establish a foundation for transforming your life, to escape your current situation and self-imposed barriers, and to see your life as limitless. I believe you can fly. Through dreaming, you can soar above and beyond to get a glimpse of and then experience a world of accomplishments, achievements, happiness, and success.

We can define dreams as ways of forming images of what we desire. When we think about our desires, they will inspire us with passion and arouse strong, positive emotions. They will transfer us to other places, take our breath away, and carry us from our daily reality. Dreams are very powerful in that they ignite vision, which is the catalyst of success. First you dream, and then you visualize achieving that dream. If you can't visualize your dream, you won't recognize it when it's there.

Your dream fueled by your desire creates your destination. Without dreaming and knowing what it is you desire, you can't create a plan or a path to achieve it. Here are the three basic steps involved in uncovering your dreams.

## Rediscover the Raw Excitement and Desire at Your Core

We were all unfiltered, raw emotions once upon a time. We laughed at what was funny and cried at what was painful. Our emotions were pure; we had no hesitation or thoughts of how we looked to others. It was the same with our passions. Our favorite toys would occupy us for hours that felt like a blink of the eye. I used to play basketball all day, sunup to sundown; I would lose track of time. I was exercising and getting better as a player, but it seemed the furthest thing from work.

Over time, however, we all started doing things we had to instead of what we wanted to, and little by little, we unknowingly pushed our joys and passions further into the distance. So the first thing we must do is uncover just what makes us happy and what we used to be excited about.

## Be the Picasso—Paint Your Future on the Canvas of Your Life

Simply choose what you want your life to look like. When you ask most people about their dreams, they won't be able to tell you and will have to think about it, or they will rattle of several things in all directions and change them because they will be undecided.

Many people just don't know their dreams because they stopped dreaming. You will have to decide what yours are. Everyone's painting will look a little different because people have different desires. This is where your dreams take flight; you can close your eyes and instantly be in another place.

Some may dream of a large mansion and acres of land, a ranch with horses, or a penthouse in a high-rise complete with doorman. Others may dream of a modest home all paid for, a loving wife, kids, and a dog. Still others may dream of exploring different destinations all over the world or being philanthropists who assist any number of charities. Whatever it may be, it will start with a passionate desire deep inside.

Start by writing down all the things you love to do, places where you want to go, and hobbies you want to indulge in—things you'd never get tired of.

## Discover Your Sense of Purpose

Imagine waking up and doing something that gave you an amazing, unwavering sense of purpose. You could do it from dusk till dawn and never get tired of it. If you had all the money in the world, what would you do for free? This sense of purpose is something you would be so passionate about. It would not be work—it would be your life.

All successful people end up trying to satisfy internal needs. No matter how much money and fame they have, if they didn't have a sense of purpose, they would feel unfulfilled.

## Don't Suppress your Dreams

If dreaming is so important, why do the majority of people not follow through or stop trying to fulfill their dreams? Among the many reasons and circumstances responsible for this, a few stand out.

## *Lack of Confidence*

You can lack confidence in what you're doing or wanting to do, and you can also lack confidence in yourself. You have to believe in your dream or you can easily get knocked off course due to others' negativity or due to the inevitable downs you'll experience. You can gain confidence, however, in multiple ways. You can study those who became successful against the odds. You can create small successes every day and little by little gain confidence in what you're doing. If you're suffering from a personal lack of confidence, you will need to grow personally, which also takes many forms. This is an important factor in success and has been concluded as such for years. In "Characteristics of Successful Entrepreneurs," an article in a Creative Education Foundation publication, David McClelland concluded that individual scholars, workshops, and institutions have come up lists of the personal characteristics of entrepreneurs. Over twenty years ago, Hal Pickle reviewed this literature for the US Small Business Administration and arrived at a list of twenty-seven characteristics that promote success in small businesses. Hornaday, Bunker, and the East-West Center Technology and Development Institute compiled very similar results. In preparation for the research reported below, McBer and Company collated the findings from seven such lists to see which characteristics were mentioned most often and to get as complete an inventory of such traits as possible.

Forty-two characteristics were mentioned by at least two sources, and a large number were on the majority of the lists. One of the most frequently mentioned traits was confidence—you either believe a hundred percent in what you're doing or you'll find it difficult to reach true success and easier to suppress your dreams. The great thing to know about this is that it's all between your ears. This book will help control the voice in your head so you can have a fighting chance. Remember, as Henry Ford stated, "Whether you think you can or not, you're right."

## Negativity and Criticism

When others try to steal your dream, remember that it's not theirs to steal—it's yours to lose. Don't let people steal your hopes just because they may not have any of their own. It's common for dreamers to be criticized when they're going for things while others around them are happy just where they are. All famous people received negativity and criticism along their journeys to success. Your critics have their own baggage; don't take ownership of it—leave it with them. This is your dream, not theirs, and to achieve your dream, you need to own it and not give negativity and criticism any power over it.

## Dreaming Dreams That Aren't Yours

If your dream or vision isn't really true to your heart, your commitment to it will suffer. An American Psychological Association study showed that the emotional well-being of someone who pursued a goal incongruent with his or her motives declined significantly; the commitment to and pursuit of a goal won't be the same and probably won't last if it's not in line with what you want. When pursuing your dream, make sure you have accurately assessed the level of importance of that dream and what it means to you.

## Setbacks

In your journey to success, it's a given that you will suffer setbacks. The important thing here is not the setbacks but how you react to them.

## Quitting before Achieving

The most disastrous reason people give up on their dreams is that they quit before they've even had a chance to succeed. This should be obvious, but when people get overwhelmed with some of the ways their dreams can be suppressed, they start forming new realities in their heads. When they start ventures but lack confidence, receive criticism from others about them, have setbacks, and are afraid of failing, they tend to start thinking it won't work, and they quit.

Out of all the reasons, this is the one you can potentially control the most. When I was on my journey to play professional basketball, all these reasons were in my face all the time. Though it was tough, I didn't quit. I often think about how my life would have been so different if I had quit. I wouldn't have experienced the life I lived in the NBA. The amazing places I traveled to, the people I met, and the experiences I enjoyed are forever branded in my mind. Playing with and getting to know Michael Jordan, Charles Barkley, and many other great players gave me the chance to engage in meaningful conversations that instilled values and shaped my future. Most important, I wouldn't have met my wife while playing with the Phoenix Suns. What if we hadn't met? My amazing son wouldn't have been born, and all the joy and laughter we have experienced wouldn't have happened.

When you're seeking success, quitting is not an option. Think of all the amazing things that wouldn't have happened or been discovered if the people who dreamed of them had quit. The lightbulb would not be here if it weren't the determination and dream of Thomas A. Edison, quoted as saying, "Many of life's failures are people who did not realize how close they were to success when they gave up."

Edison had been told by a teacher, "You're too stupid to learn anything." He was fired from his first two jobs for being nonproductive. As an inventor, he made one thousand attempts before he successfully created the lightbulb. A reporter asked him, "How does it feel to have failed a thousand times?" Edison answered, "I didn't fail a thousand times. The lightbulb was an invention with a thousand steps." Edison said, "A man should mentally mark out a straight pathway to achievement, looking neither to the right or to the left, but straight."

Most successful people like Edison will tell you the journey to success is not perfect or easy. Some achievers had to face being told they didn't have the qualities needed for success.

## Fear of Failing

The fear of failing is probably the biggest reason people quit on their dreams. This fact proves the old saying that we are our worst enemies, but we have more control than we think. The physical feeling we get when we're fearful can compromise our actual performance. Even in its simplest forms, fear can cause changes in our bodies. Unlike the excitement dreams can create, fear can cause negative emotions.

We've all had moments when we were nervous and so worked up about doing something simple; in our minds, we made it a lot bigger deal that it really was. A person's physiological makeup can change the outcome of his or her performance, and we call a common form of it "choking," a physical reaction to a psychological situation. The fear of not performing well or failing is the usual reason for choking, and this can apply to taking tests, speaking in front of people, or shooting a game-winning free throw. Fear can affect us physically; our breathing can get short and our muscles tighten when the results we're trying to achieve are important and our performance really matters. The fear of failing can have an incredible impact on people. It's been said that people rank their fear of public speaking above their fear of dying!

The fear usually comes from past memories or situations in which the person didn't perform well right when they're faced with a similar situation or challenge. When someone remembers not having performed well, this can make succeeding at that task seem impossibly difficult. But we just have to remember that it's all in the head. In a later chapter, I will write about how to properly understand and overcome such fear-producing negative thoughts.

## Dreams Have Power

Thomas Jefferson said, "I like the dreams of the future better than the history of the past." Dreams can be very powerful. They're the reason some people work up to twenty hours a day, sleep for just four, and never seem tired. They're fired up by their dreams, and they achieve their dreams through their passion. Some people pursue their dreams for years before realizing them, but they never gave up. No matter what their age, they visualized their dreams, knowing that would give them a better chance of achieving them. Many ordinary people of all ages and walks of life have achieved extraordinary things because they had dreams and the vision to pursue them relentlessly.

One young man desired success. He worked many different jobs, from piloting a boat to selling insurance, but all with minimal success. When he turned forty, he began serving chicken dinners at a service station he started. Over the next several years, he developed a way to pressure-fry chicken that became a hit with his customers. He opened a restaurant just in the right place at the right time; some have said he was plain lucky. But luck is just preparation meeting opportunity. His restaurant right off a freeway became a huge success. He became so busy that he started franchising, and Kentucky Fried chicken was born. Colonel Sanders was sixty-five when he fulfilled his dream.

Don't underestimate the power of your dreams. They may help you develop skill sets you never knew you had or could develop, and you never know when vision can be harnessed to opportunity. In 1954, Ray Kroc was fifty-two when he started McDonald's. Most people that age think about retiring. One day while selling milkshake machines, he visited a hamburger stand in San Bernardino, California. What he saw ignited a dream that became one of the greatest success stories in history. Instead of selling the McDonald brothers his machine, he bought the business, and the rest is history.

Ray Kroc became a pioneer in the fast-food industry with his ideas of making food preparation more efficient. He created a uniform system of producing hamburgers, milkshakes, and french fries so the food tasted the same in each McDonald's.

By 1960, he had more than two hundred McDonald's franchises in the United States. He started national advertising to support the franchises, he bought property to lease to them, and he expanded across the country and the globe. McDonald's, a great success, is often the model for fast-food establishments.

## Dreams Can Foster Change

The Rev. Martin Luther King Jr. delivered a speech on August 28, 1963, at the Lincoln Memorial in Washington, DC, "I Have a Dream," one of the most acclaimed speeches ever. It endures as one of the defining moments in the civil rights movement and is still heralded as a beacon in the ongoing struggle for racial equality. It has inspired the start of numerous organizations, associations, movements, and more. The reach and impact of the words he spoke that day have been global.

In an article in the Huffington Post, Nicholas Wapshott wrote about the reach of King's speech. King couldn't have guessed his name would be commandeered by all, including liberal white politicians who even created the Martin Luther King Adventure Playground in Islington, North London, to boost their credentials. BBC broadcasts a "we are the world" iteration by having world leaders, peacemakers, and protesters read parts of King's speech to an estimated 239 million around the world.

King's soaring close, "Let freedom ring," resonates today and inspires those who are moved by his dream as stated by author Gary Younge, who wrote the book *The Speech*.

Every great achievement started with a dream. For your future success, it's imperative you understand and not overlook this crucial step and not underestimate its power. Sometimes, dreams are so intense that people can be swept off their feet by them and forget their present reality.

Why are dreams so powerful? They can cause us to visualize the lives we want. Thomas Edison, Colonel Sanders, Ray Kroc, and Dr. Martin Luther King had bigger-than-life dreams but also the vision to see, internalize, map them out, and take action to make them happen.

Visualizing a dream is a matter of replaying a mental movie of your desired outcome; it will become a guide that will keep you on the track toward your dream.

## Visualization

Visualizing your dreams can actually cause emotional and chemical changes you will feel. Create a movie in your mind of your desired outcome—pictures and a soundtrack that involve all your senses. I used this often when I played and still do today. I recall mentally running scenarios of the perfect game. I imagined releasing the ball and watching it floating through the air and into the hoop—swish!

If your dream was winning a marathon, you would visualize the scenery passing by, smell the fresh air, feel the warm sun, and spot the finish line. You would feel the ribbon connect with your torso and watch your feet cross the line. You would hear the crowd cheering your victory. Such mental movies can become so real that you'll hate coming back to reality.

Top performers and high achievers use this technique as a part of their daily training regimens. Visualizing has been around for a long time; it has evolved and is now a common "mental prescription" utilized by top trainers and coaches of peak performance. In an interview, sports psychologist Richard Suinn, PhD, who in 1972 became the first psychologist to serve on the US Olympic medicine team and headed the American Psychological Association, spoke about the evolution of sports psychology. He said it was originally used to identify those athletes who had the potential to become superior at their sports. Modern sports psychology focuses more on mental training and exercises that strengthen mental skills such as stress management, visualization, goal setting, concentration, focus, and even relaxation.

In my quest to make it in professional sports, I was told that when I got to that level, everyone would be a great athlete and the playing field would be level. What separates athletes who become successful is their mental strength—how well they can see themselves accomplishing their desired outcomes. Performance is 10 percent physical and 90 percent mental, though many think it's the other way around. Techniques such as guided imagery and mental rehearsal can increase an athlete's efficiency and effectiveness. In pro sports, winning and losing can be separated by milliseconds—a small margin makes a world of difference.

I have had some amazing influences who prove this point. Phil Jackson, who has eleven NBA Championships under his leadership with such teams as the Bulls and the Lakers, is a shining example of the power of visualization and the power of the mind to accomplish dreams. Jackson is known for his approach to coaching that was influenced by Eastern philosophy; he was given the nickname "Zen Master" for this reason. He credited this concept as a major guiding force in his life.

His approach was amazing. He was calm, and unlike most coaches, he never yelled at his players. The environment he created felt very controlled; his players' focus was on performance and mentally controlling the desired outcome. He had the ability to transfer his attitude to his players; when we played, we expected to win.

My pregame preparation included players' standard actions, including shoot-arounds, watching films, stretching, and resting. At that point, we were all in shape, but what made a big difference was our visualization of the results. I would see the free throw line and the players lined up; I would see the crowd behind the backboard anticipating the shot I was about to make. I could feel the ball in my hands and the sweat running down my face as I began to release the ball. I heard nothing; I saw the ball rotating and going over the rim. Swoosh. Nothing but net. I saw the spectators rise to their feet with a thunderous roar. I just won the game. After such visualization, when the situation was actually happening, I felt comfortable; I had been there before.

Whether in business, sports, or even difficult situations people find themselves in, the power of the mind and mental rehearsal have proven to be valuable assets. In his autobiography, Nelson Mandela wrote extensively on how visualization helped him keep a positive attitude while he was imprisoned for twenty-seven years. He dreamed of the day he would be released. "I thought continually of the day when I would walk free. I fantasized about what I would do."

Visualization of dreams is not only a mental activity; it can produce actual physical changes as well. Your thoughts are connected to your body through your senses, particularly sight and sound. Have you ever been excited about something and gotten goose bumps as a result? Have you ever seen something that scared you or freaked you out, such as a car crash, a horror movie, or a rodent, and sent chills up your spine?

Your brain's reaction to such stimuli, good or bad, causes chemical changes in your body. The emotional center of the brain, the hypothalamus, transforms emotions into physical responses. The chemical effect linking your mind to your body through your organs, hormones, and cellular activity is controlled by neuropathies. Whether you visualize negative or positive outcomes, your body and possibly your outcome will follow that lead. This process has also been known to promote healing; we've all heard of the placebo effect. Don't underestimate the power of your mind, and don't take it for granted.

As we go through the remainder of my ten principles, I encourage you to take notes and answer key questions that arise. At the end of each chapter are exercises that apply to each principle. Take time to answer the questions before reading on.

## Exercise Drills to Uncover Your Dreams

 What were your childhood or high school dreams? (Don't think about this too judgmentally; just write down as many dreams as you can remember from then no matter how unrealistic they seem.)

 What were your dreams years ago? What are they today?

 How have they evolved? In what ways have they just been pushed to the side?

If you were to rewrite one of your dreams with the insight of an adult but the optimism of a child, what would your new dreams be?

 Write down at least three things or people who epitomize your aspirations and help you focus on your dream.

# CHAPTER

# MAKE THE CHOICE
# TO BE SUCCESSFUL

## *Commit to Win*

*Every choice you make has an end result.*
—Zig Ziglar

A FEW THINGS ABOUT SUCCESSFUL PEOPLE STAND OUT: THEIR TALENTS AND the choices they make. When these are combined, amazing things result. Quite often, you will see people with extreme talent who nonetheless struggle for success. That's because talent alone is not the answer; it has to be combined with the ability to make the right choices without constant deliberation. People who constantly second-guess themselves can become victims of analysis paralysis. They start kicking the can down the road to avoid making the choice to move forward. Before you can become successful at any endeavor, you must first make the choice to do so.

Life is nothing but a series of choices, and the choices you make will define who you are and what you become. Before you can become successful yourself and thereby have a positive impact on others, you must make the *choice* to do so. Maybe you've heard this a million times and listened with half an ear to what sounds like obvious, easy advice, but regardless of its apparent simplicity, the failure to choose success is a major stumbling block for millions; way too many people struggle with this principle.

People have heard the phrase *Make the choice* so much that they've become numb to it, but making a choice requires mental action. You can ponder matters for days, years, weeks, or decades, but actually choosing sets a direction. Timing is heavily involved in the game of life. Certain situations require making timely choices that may decide what we dream about, the direction of our futures, and the outcome.

I had a choice to make about retiring early or waiting a few years. By making a firm and timely choice, I was able to take advantage of the real estate boom that lasted six years; I made millions. If I would've waited, I would have started off in real estate right at the beginning of the economy's crash, which would have pushed the entire process ahead over a decade. I wouldn't have had the experience, knowledge, or the years of earning at a high capacity.

Choosing success means giving yourself permission to be successful. If I asked you face-to-face whether you deserved success, your answer would be yes, but most people don't believe deep down they deserve success. Each negative experience, each failure, gets recorded on your private "lowlights" reel and plays repeatedly in your subconscious and maybe even in your conscious mind.

Focusing on your failures will make you feel unfit for success, but true success is a journey of wins and losses. To start winning again, you have to be brave enough to make the choice to succeed. If you avoid doing what's necessary to achieve a goal or a desired outcome, you're also making the choice to fail whether you realize it or not.

Our choices are usually based on our life goals. One difficult choice I was faced with impacted who I was going to be for the rest of my life. I was supposed to be drafted into the NBA, but I wasn't; there were so many great players who came out that year that I was pushed out. I could have accepted defeat and started looking at other career options, but I made the choice to pursue basketball; there was no going back for me. I was going to make it happen.

I called several agents and heard from people in Chicago who said they wanted to make some calls on my behalf. I was extremely excited; I elevated my workouts to get ready for the trip. When I arrived at my meeting, instead of agents giving me a multiyear NBA contract (they said the NBA team under consideration was going in another direction), they told me of a lucrative offer from a European basketball team that wanted me to fly out ASAP. I had become good friends with the assistant who had been assigned to take care of me during my stay in Chicago; in the days leading up to my meeting, we discovered we had a lot in common. When the agents broke the news about the failed NBA deal to me, the assistant gave me a strange look. While the others were out rounding up the documentation for the European team, the assistant pulled me aside and told me not to sign anything until he could talk to me in private. We stepped outside. He said, "Joe! I have to be honest with you. The NBA team didn't turn you down! The agents get paid 3 percent commission if you accept the NBA deal but 15 percent if you accept the European deal!"

I was infuriated and disgusted. I made a tough choice. I went back to the meeting, looked the agents in their eyes, and said, "You don't define me, and you never will. I came here to play in the NBA, and that's what I'm going to do." I terminated them on the spot.

> You might well remember that nothing can
> bring you success but yourself.
> —Dr. Napoleon Hill

## Choices Can Change the Direction of Your Life

I'm sure such an experience has happened to plenty of other players, and some version of it has likely happened to you. You were presented with some lesser version of your dream and were pressured to take it; what you were told was supposed to be your only option. I was certainly terrified I had indeed just turned down my only option, my only offer to play professional sports, and I was afraid it could well have been my last. But even through the fear, I knew I had to stick to my guns and hold out for the real thing. My dream was the NBA, and I was all in.

The assistant who'd warned me about the shady deal ended up leaving to start his own agency because of his former bosses' lack of integrity. We got together to talk about my options. He wanted to help me land a new deal. In the meantime, since we were in Chicago, I asked him, "Where do the NBA players work out?" Maybe if I went there, I thought, I could get noticed. He dropped me off at the Chicago Athletic Club. That turned out to be one of the defining moments of my career.

I walked into the second-floor gym; NBA players I was used to seeing on TV were mixing with other hopefuls such as myself. I laced up my shoes and started playing. I just kept thinking, *I'm going to get noticed. I'm going to carve my own way.* I had nothing to lose, so I played as hard as I could. I held my own even against seasoned NBA players, and I was starting to get attention from the guys on court. What I didn't know was that I was getting attention from off the court too.

After the game, a personal trainer who'd been on the sidelines told me he thought I had a lot of talent but also a lot of anger. If I could learn to channel the anger and the energy into productive plays, I could probably be something in the NBA. I asked who he was. He answered, "You'll find out soon enough."

He wanted to know why I was there, and I didn't hesitate to tell him I was trying to make it into the NBA. He brightened; he told me to meet him there at seven the next morning to show him what I was made of.

Long before morning came, I found out I had spoken with Tim Grover, Michael Jordon's personal trainer. I was simultaneously ecstatic and sick with nerves. Michael Jordan's personal trainer had just watched me putting it out all on the floor as if I had had nothing to lose. He wanted to see more!

The next morning, I showed up, laced my shoes, and got ready for work. We worked through some drills for about forty-five minutes before Tim told me to take a break; he said my workout partner would be arriving in a few minutes. As I waited on the sidelines, the elevator opened. Michael Jordan stepped out. Every life has pivot points, and that moment was one of the most pivotal in my entire life. Nothing has ever been the same since.

Why is choice so important? A choice defines and sets in motion an all-out, no-quit path until you reach your destination. It clearly defines one option out of many. When you make a definitive choice, the universe hears you and pauses for a moment. From that point on, your actions define your choices. As mentioned earlier, some people decide or say they're going to do something but start overthinking, deliberating, and second-guessing themselves even with everyday decisions.

CHAPTER TWO

A study that appeared in *Science* magazine reported on experiments with student volunteers and real-life shoppers that suggest too much contemplation gets in the way of good decision making, especially when the choice is complicated. Though choosing to be successful shouldn't be a complicated decision, the process of how people come to conclusions about matters can affect their level of confidence and commitment to what they choose. The study revealed that even though most people think that deliberating consciously is the way to make choices, it is not always the best way to go. The deliberation-without-attention hypothesis holds that the more complex and important the choice, the less conscious deliberation and the more unconscious thought one should put into it. Simple choices—for instance, deciding to use oven mitts rather than towels—work better with conscious thought. But choosing between different houses or cars is more instinctual and uses unconscious thought.

## Choice vs. Decision

I differentiate between "choices" and "decisions." As far as taking your life above the rim is concerned, a choice is the act of selecting between two or more possibilities. The higher the stakes, the more important it is for you to make the right choices; they will become your road map to success or failure. Decisions, on the other hand, are based on the present with little consideration for the impact they will have on the future.

You can often tell the difference between a choice and a decision by listening to the way you talk about it. Decisions come with additional language, which helps justify them. A decision might sound like, "I'm hungry and there's a party at work, so I'll have some chocolate cake." A life stitched together from a series of decisions rarely results in success because decisions don't take the long view; they're based solely on today's circumstances.

Choices on the other hand are made based not only on your circumstances today but also on your hopes for the future. Choices are never far removed from your long-term goals regardless of the circumstances of the day. A choice might sound like, "I'm hungry and there's a party at work, but I don't want to blow my progress toward my goal of losing ten pounds. Looks like there's a veggie plate that will tide me over. No chocolate cake for me!" Sorry. No one said choices would be easy. In fact, it's quite the opposite.

## The Heavy Cost of Decisions

The temporal nature of decisions leaves room for retreat and wavering if things go wrong. Making a choice is more like burning the bridge behind you, leaving no options but to succeed or die trying. That may sound dramatic, but isn't it much worse to quit on your dreams and goals and live a life in which you're dying instead of living? You were born as a unique individual to accomplish amazing things; you just have to *believe* that.

Making a choice can be very liberating. You may think you have no control over certain choices, and that tends to give you a feeling of being out of control. But even in the midst of circumstances truly beyond your control, you still have choices, and exercising your power to choose will open a new window on the world.

Let's say you were planning to go out with your partner and have a day together outside, maybe a picnic, but the sky suddenly becomes overcast and rains out your plans. You can choose to be unhappy and negative and say the rain has ruined your day, or you can look at that situation as a possibility to create something magical. Instead of complaining, you put together a cheese and hors d'oeuvres plate, pour some wine, put on some good background music, open the doors to feel a breeze, and listen to the rain create a romantic environment for you and your partner.

You had no choice about the rain, but you could choose how you responded to it; you could choose to be happy under the circumstances. We sometimes don't realize that adversity sets the stage for the choices we make that will define our lifelong greatness.

Sometimes, we don't understand that our choices can end up setting us up for greatness or not. Not all our choices will work out, but even in the midst of failure, we can hold our heads high, knowing we didn't dodge our challenges or make excuses. We didn't arrive at our places in life by default. The strength of character and the experience we gain when we attack everything life has to offer with integrity will lead to future successes.

Nothing is easier than me just telling you the importance of making a choice; actually getting down to the nitty-gritty and doing it requires more than platitudes. I offer you here five steps that will walk you through the process of making a choice to live your life above the rim.

## Five Steps to Making Definitive Choices to Live Above the Rim

### 1. Let Your Choice Be Driven by Your "Why"

Your "why" should create emotion. In some cases, people even cry when they talk about the reason they want a desired outcome. In the last chapter, you read about having a dream. If you're following the action guide, you have worked through the noise covering your forgotten dreams. Now that you've articulated your dream, think about the reasons you have them. No matter what they are, they have to be powerful and emotional. You'll need to have a burning desire to achieve your dream if you're going to withstand the challenges you'll inevitably face.

### 2. Choose the Right Vehicle for Your Destination

Choose the right career path, job, or business that will enable you to reach your goal. If you want to make a million but choose a job that doesn't give you the opportunity to do so, you're wasting your time. A waiter whose goal it is to earn a million will probably spend a great deal of time achieving that. The opportunity to make that kind of money in real estate is achievable; you just have to sell many houses or more-expensive houses. This point should be obvious, but it's one many people don't understand. Even when they've chosen to be successful, the vehicles they choose sometimes can't get them where they want to go. If my destination is to get to New York from Los Angeles and I want to drive a Ferrari, a very nice car, I might want to stop for a minute and consider my real goal: is it driving a Ferrari to New York or getting efficiently and quickly to New York? The Ferrari would get me there in several days, whereas a Boeing 747 would get me there under five hours.

Many of us choose vehicles of nine-to-five jobs—nothing wrong with that; a good job is respectable. But we need to realize that if we choose a vehicle with limited potential, we may never reach our goals. Different dreams require different career vehicles if we desire maximum potential. Is there a risk? Yes, of course. No risk, no reward; we've all heard that. Dreams are great, but if you don't have the vehicle you need to accomplish your dreams, they're going to be short-lived.

Take a look at your personal assets. This can start off being pretty frustrating. You may think, *Wow! There's no way I can accomplish the things I want with the assets currently at my disposal.* But if you break down your goals into smaller, easier-to-achieve milestones, you will make your goals more attainable. Sure, investing in a multimillion-dollar hotel may be currently out of your reach, but if that's your goal, break it into bite-sized pieces, smaller steps that will take you to your dream. As you reach each one, your vehicle becomes better and better suited to getting you all the way to success. Don't stress out that you don't seem to be equipped with the right vehicle from the start; the vehicle you begin with is not the one you're stuck with forever.

The key is to identify which step your current vehicle can get you to. Depending on your goals and your current vehicle, the first step on your journey might be a walking program, a better education, a second job, or a modest investment regimen.

The vehicle you choose has to be able to make it to your destination. Here are a few tips to know if you have the right vehicle.

- Start by identifying your dream as stated in chapter 1; that will point you in the right direction.

- Make sure your vehicle is in line with your passion.

- Make sure your vehicle doesn't limit you by being a temporary fix that can become a long-term obligation. People often get second jobs so they can pay for the resources they need to achieve their dreams, but this often leads to exhaustion and can actually limit them if the second job is more demanding than their first. Don't find yourself in a few years overworked, underpaid, exhausted, and even further from your desired outcome; short-term fixes can derail your progress.

- Make sure your vehicle allows you to acquire the skills you need.

- Make sure your vehicle makes financial sense. Put pen to paper; if it doesn't work on paper, chances are it won't work in reality.

- Make sure the vehicle rewards performance as well as provides a base income. Bonuses can really help you move faster than expected.

- Get an internship in your dream field. Hands-on experience is great for preparing you for the real thing.

## 3. Choose Only What You Truly Love

Steve Jobs said, "The only way to do great work is to love what you do" and "People with passion can change the world for the better." That's great advice from a fantastically successful entrepreneur. When you have a passion for something, it will never seem like work. And doing something you're passionate about will give you the drive to excel, and you'll be more likely to achieve financial success in addition to being thrilled about what you're doing.

## 4. Consider the Consequences of Not Choosing to Follow Your Dream

If your life always stayed the same, could you live with yourself? When you imagine yourself looking back ten, thirty, even fifty years from now, how will you feel realizing you hadn't gone for it and made the choice to change your life? Since you're reading this book, you've probably already decided you don't want to live with the regret that comes with missed opportunity.

I had an opportunity to be in the slam-dunk contest with the Phoenix Suns. I deliberated on it and got opinions from the coach and other people about taking part in the contest because it was in the middle of the season. It was at the All Star break, when most players jump at the opportunity to take some much-needed rest. I was just starting to play well and had really started to define who I was in my career, so I was hesitant to take part in the contest. I thought if I didn't enter the contest, there was always next year. I decided against the slam dunk contest; I wanted to save energy and be fresh so I could end the season well in the playoffs.

That decision turned out to be one of the most pivotal decisions I have ever made; that year, I could've won the contest, gained notoriety, and catapulted my NBA career. I never had the same opportunity again.

Most of the choices we make daily are not about such contests, but in my life, this stands out. When your mind declines to make a choice to follow a dream but your heart really wants to, it will haunt you forever. Year after year, I saw this as a missed opportunity to have done something great. Till this day, it's one of my decisions I've regretted the most. I decided the choices that I made in my life were going to be those I would stand behind when my heart said so. It's much better to deal with the consequences knowing that you feel completely fulfilled rather than being hesitant to make a choice and regretting it forever. We all have choices at every juncture of our lives, and making this or that choice might not change your life overnight, but it will change the direction of your life and drive you to fulfillment and happiness without regrets.

Those who decide to be successful start living life at that moment instead of life living them. They wake up excited, with butterflies in their stomachs; each day for them is an opportunity to experience something amazing and new in their journeys to success.

You can spend the rest of your life living or the rest of your life dying; it's your choice!

## 5. Declaration

After you've gone through steps one through four, you should be at a point to know you're making a choice, but it's just not good enough to think about it—you have to firmly declare the choice you've made. Later on in this book, you'll read about the transformational power of declaration, the ultimate step in making a choice. Without a declaration, a choice has not been made.

Declaration is the step that burns the bridge; there's no turning back. Too many people have one foot in and one foot out, never able to give a hundred percent toward their goals. They will never be able to get the most out of themselves. They'll be living in unstable mental and physical environments, constantly second-guessing themselves.

## Find a Way to Believe

If your choice is in line with all five steps, you can be confident it was the right choice. You've uncovered your dream and chosen to be successful. But after you make the choice, you have to believe you deserve it, but that's easier said than done, right? If you don't believe you deserve success, you'll always quit on yourself before great things happen. All too often, nonbelief comes from a lack of confidence. Changing your confidence won't happen overnight, but with the right tools, you can rebuild your damaged confidence and refuel your belief in yourself. In chapter 5, you'll discover keys to revealing the thief that's been stealing your confidence, and you'll learn ways to control it—for good.

## Exercise Drills for Making a Choice

*Clarify your goal or objectives.* You have to consider the whole picture. Making a choice is not just to satisfy an isolated component but also a broader view and how the choice affects your desired outcome for the future. Define and write out what you expect to gain.

 *Collect all applicable data.* Get all the facts and figures you need to make a choice, including spreadsheets, studies, feedback, or examples of people who have made the same choice. Look to your own mental and emotional data that will affect your desired outcome. People often make choices based on limited information, and that can lead to bad choices. Don't let a lack of information hinder you from making a choice. Write down what it will take to reach your goal such as time needed, money required, and different ways to achieve your goal.

***Decide on a reward for achieving your goal.*** It's critical to define the reward you'll derive from reaching your goal. What will your life be like when you achieve it? This is where you can take a minute to dream and visualize as mentioned in chapter 1. Your "why" should be involved in this process. Write out the benefit you'll receive from achieving your goal financially and emotionally, and post it where you can see it daily.

 ***Think of the consequences of not making a choice.*** What will your life be like if you don't choose to achieve your goal? A lot of clarity will come from your answer to this question. Understanding the impact of not choosing to go for your goal is very sobering; the regret could haunt you forever. Write down the financial and emotional consequences you'll face for failing to choose and how they will affect your family and future. When you're having a bad day or feeling like quitting, read it!

***Review and declare.*** After reviewing all the information, you should be in a place where you are more comfortable making the choice. But the most important thing you can do short of making the choice is declaring it.

Review these steps above and declare your desired outcome by writing it down and verbally reciting it.

# CHAPTER

# SET EXPECTATIONS

## Prepare for Your Season with the Correct Mind-Set

*The expectations of life depend upon diligence; the mechanic*
*that would perfect his work must first sharpen his tools.*
—Confucius

AFTER I MADE THE CHOICE TO FOLLOW MY DREAM OF BECOMING AN NBA player, I studied and watched many interviews with people who'd already made it. Without exception, they talked about how much work they had put in it. "Pistol Pete" Maravich dribbled a ball every day, everywhere he went, up and down the hallways—even along railroad tracks. Magic Johnson kept a ball with him all the time; he even slept with it. Michael Jordan put in hours of practice well above and beyond the required team practices and workouts.

Because successful players were so open about all the hard work and dedication it took to get them to the top of their game, my expectations were realistic from early on. When I picked up a basketball for the first time, I knew mastering it was going to take *work*. Because I was prepared for that, I was willing to do whatever it took; my mind was fixed on the prize. I stayed after school, I practiced in the evenings, I dribbled the basketball every time I had the chance, and I played as much as I could. I was willing to do whatever it took to become a pro. Spoiler alert! I eventually made it, and I know now that every minute spent running, lifting weights, and dribbling was worth it.

When I finally made it to the NBA, I learned it wasn't good enough just to be there; with success came a whole new set of expectations. I could no longer excel just by being a tall, fit athlete. Everybody in the NBA fit that description at the bare minimum; most of them were taller, and they were all great athletes. If I was going to play and stay in the league, the already intense work ethic that had gotten me there wasn't going to be enough. I couldn't just put in the hours; they had to be the

43

most efficient and effective hours they could be. I had the same number of hours in the day that all other talented people around me had. If I didn't leverage those hours to their fullest potential, I wasn't going to be able to make it.

One of the ways I made that happen was by soliciting the help of Tim Grover, whom you will remember from the previous chapter as Michael Jordan's personal trainer and the man who helped me break into the NBA. Tim was the best. He set my expectations properly and let me know right from the beginning the amount of work we needed to put in. We had constant structure. I had milestones so I could see where I was along the way toward my goals. Realistic expectations were a key part of why I was able to earn my first NBA position with the Bulls as well as positions on six teams after the Bulls.

I don't believe in luck. Preparation and opportunity meet, and they certainly did in my case. But I don't mind telling you that playing with the Bulls that year, I felt pretty lucky, preparation and opportunity notwithstanding.

## Get Real from the Start

Setting expectations for yourself, your environment, and your organization can be the difference between succeeding and quitting, between winning and losing. The road to success is not free of challenges, and one of the main reasons people quit on their goals is because they don't set correct expectations. Success doesn't just take work, it takes *hard* work—sacrifice, dedication, dealing with adversity, and commitment. You have to develop the correct mind-set to endure and see your goals to their completion. When you set realistic expectations, you set yourself up with the mind-set to endure.

## Why Are Realistic Expectations So Important?

First off, realistic expectations eliminate surprises; there's nothing worse than a bait-and-switch. Just imagine someone telling you a blender cost $39.99, but when you went to pay, you heard, "Oh yeah, I forgot to tell you about tax. And we also have markup. Plus we have some fees on top of that." If you really had your heart set on that blender, you might buy it, but you'd still be disgusted with the sales tactics, and your trust in the store would evaporate. When you set the wrong expectations, even if your intentions were good, it really can ruin a relationship fast whether that relationship is with a goal, with people, or with yourself.

Second, going into something without knowing what it takes will set you up to fail. People often give up because they started with the wrong expectations. If you don't know what you're in for, you're likely to be discouraged the first time you hit a bump. You'll read hardships as failures rather than as mere obstacles, and you'll probably quit long before you achieve results. With realistic expectations, however, you will more easily recognize that your journey will be a bit of a roller coaster. Some days you'll have ups, and other days there'll be downs; you'll experience excitement and disappointment. However, with a stable, balanced approach and an eye on the distant prize, you'll make it through.

Third, expectations provide a great framework. Take marathoners, for example, who know that at mile one, they will feel pretty good; they're just getting warmed up. At mile number four, they're still feeling okay but might start feeling the run a bit. By mile nine, they're prepared to be a little bit tired. After that, they know they will hit their personal walls, but they also know that at mile twenty, they'll get that second wind and cruise on home.

The wrong way to set up expectations is to tell yourself, *It's a marathon. I can do it. I'll get plenty of sleep, go all out, and win this race.* That's setting the wrong expectations. They're ambitious, exciting, and positive, but they won't prepare you for the challenges you'll face. When you hit the wall unprepared, you'll be more likely to quit than to push to the reward.

Fourth, working under the wrong expectations often results in wasted time and energy. Imagine working on a project for six months only be told your expectations had been wrong from the start, that all your work up to that point needed to be tossed out and that you had to start over. That's depressing, but it can often be avoided by starting with reasonable expectations.

## Tools for Setting Realistic Expectations

### *Develop a Long-Term Vision*

Taking the long view sets the right tone. Anything that's worth working for is probably going to take a significant amount of time to achieve. There are no get-rich-quick schemes in your future.

### *Work on Your Work Ethic*

Dreams take work. This is probably one of my favorites. Wouldn't it be awesome if something flew down with a magic potion and said, "Take this magic potion and you'll be successful overnight." We all know that's not realistic. Success takes work, but the good news is that it's just work!

### *Follow Footsteps on the Trail*

Whatever your goal may be, chances are someone has attempted it before and has succeeded or failed at it. Studying people who have already succeeded can teach you valuable lessons. The experiences of people who didn't make it can be equally as valuable. The contrast in both can create parameters or guidelines that may prepare you for your journey.

In 1993, I went to the NBA Summer League to be noticed by agents, scouts, and coaches. That's a path hundreds of players take every year, and it's proven to be a good move for many. I had a choice to go to minicamp with one of the NBA teams and fight it out with the others—five to ten guys competing for one spot. I'd noticed in previous leagues that summer that all players would do whatever it took to get on the team but when game time came, they would all be on the bench most of the game and would play little if any. If I wanted to get noticed, I couldn't chance sitting on the bench, so I improvised. I reviewed what I had seen and studied before and decided to be on the free-agent team made up of players who hadn't been accepted to the summer camp with one of the NBA teams but would play against them each game. Some players thought I was crazy for making that choice, but I knew this would be my chance to really show what I had because I would likely play the entire game. I'd have plenty of time on the court to showcase myself.

The plan worked. Every game, I put up great numbers. I averaged thirty points and even shot fifty-seven once against players who were contract NBA players who played regularly during the season. I'd never have gotten that opportunity if I'd based my expectations on what I had learned from others.

## Know Your Availability

How much time can you commit, and how much time are you willing to commit to your goal? This is a big one; not understanding how much time you can or are willing to commit can lead to overcommitting, which leads to frustration, which of course can lead to quitting. Set your expectations correctly by determining how much time you have and how much you can put toward a certain goal or achievement. Even if it takes you longer than you thought, you'll be a lot happier and will set yourself up for success. You'll be able to achieve that goal.

## Develop a Routine

Evaluating your daily schedule is another big concern; it helps you determine how much time you can realistically commit compared to what you'll need to do on a daily basis to accomplish your goals.

When I was playing pro sports or working toward other goals, I always set a deadline for myself. If I set a goal for six weeks, I understood it might not end up being exactly six weeks, but at least I had a framework to build on. I'd work my way backward from that self-imposed deadline and create a daily schedule that mapped out the route to my goal.

Technology is very handy when it comes to creating timelines and sticking to routines. People are over 90 percent more successful remembering things if they write them down. If you set aside time in your daily schedule to work toward your goal, add it as an appointment on your computer, tablet, smartphone—or all three—along with a reminder alarm. Whether it's for exercise sessions, writing, making phone calls to network, or anything that you've decided to dedicate time to, daily and weekly schedules with earmarked time will keep your expectations realistic and on track. How successful do you imagine you'd be if you said, "I'm going to be a doctor" but didn't change your daily or weekly schedule to include time for working toward that goal? It would be pretty tough to achieve without understanding the time commitment it was going to take.

## Expect Highs and Lows

The roller-coaster ride is another huge issue. If you're prepared for the ups and downs from the start, you won't be as susceptible to disappointment when you have your mental seat belt on for the inevitable dips in the road. It's not a matter of *if* but *when* you'll experience highs and lows in any challenging endeavor, but what's important is how fast you recover from them.

Being durable has its advantages; if you are prepared for setbacks up front, you will be able to outlast those who are less prepared and more likely to throw in the towel. I've seen this happen in all types of businesses, from corporate environments to home-based endeavors. This can be especially true about people in network marketing. Many people don't have their expectations set properly and think they can get rich overnight, but it doesn't quite work that way, and they quit before they can get their reward.

## Show Me the Money (or Not)

Depending on the business and the industry, it could take only a few months for you to start turning a profit on a new endeavor, or it could take years. If you go in to a business financially unprepared, you may not just get discouraged—you may get shut out early because your funds dry up. That's not to say there are some things you just shouldn't go for. Instead, you need to put in the research and planning to be prepared for what your endeavor will take. If you put all your personal savings into a business and absolutely must start earning a profit in a year but your business will realistically not be financially viable for three years, you won't last long enough to see success.

## Exercise Drills to Set Expectations

 **Expectations:** Write down the potential highs and lows you can expect from the journey to your goal.

 **Limitations:** What limitations do you have to overcome to achieve your goal? Money, negativity, time, distance, etc.? Write these down.

 **Timelines:** What is your minimum and maximum timeline for achieving your goal?

 **Budgets:** If you need additional income to achieve your goal, how much will that be? How will you get it? Whatever figure you come up with, add 30 percent.

# CHAPTER

# IDENTIFY YOUR RIMS

## *Know Your Limits*

*Once we accept our limits, we go beyond them.*
—Albert Einstein

**W**HAT IS YOUR "RIM"? IT'S YOUR PERSONAL GLASS CEILING, THE LIMIT OR barrier that represents the level above which you will not succeed. Your rim is the sum of what you believe you can achieve and what your environment says you can achieve. The good news is that your rim is a moveable target. You can elevate it and break through to new heights. The bad news is that you can also inadvertently lower it as you shrink yourself and your aspirations to fit the negativity in and around you.

When I set out to play professional basketball, I knew it would be difficult, but I worked hard. Along the way, I had to rise above several rims. First, I had to conquer my psychological limitations, the voices inside that questioned whether I could do it. But after I broke the backboard on that barrier (with positive feedback from myself and from my mother), there was still another rim in its place—my environment. I had so much negativity around me. Everybody was telling me, "You can't make it. Do you know how few people make it to the NBA? You've got a better chance of being struck by lightning." Those were just some of the negative comments that came my way.

If I had submerged myself in those comments day in and day out, they would have translated into thoughts in my head and I probably would have quit. Instead, I found ways to replace those voices. Replacing them became an ongoing challenge because negative voices continued to follow me even into college. People continued to share their unsolicited negative opinions with me (how generous of them!).

My peers expressed negativity about my dreams, but they themselves were also quitting on their dreams, and quitters love company. The rim my environment had created was being reinforced on all sides. I had to find a way to defeat it and fast. Within a few years, I was either going to be working a full-time job or playing as one of the top 365 players in the world on an NBA court. I had to find a way to conquer the environmental rim created by the negative voices around me.

## Overcoming the Negatives

I approached the rim from every angle. Not only did I build up my psychological reinforcements by reading, dreaming, positive affirmation, confirmation, and envisioning, I also started doing extra work. I got up in the middle of the night. I started running. I got into the best shape of my life because I knew if I could replace the negativity with something tangibly positive, I had a better chance of keeping my dreams alive.

My method worked. My confidence grew, and it elevated the level of my rim.

To build an environment filled with positive rather than negative people, I started talking to classmates who were going to be drafted in the NBA and the NFL. I surrounded myself with players who were focused, driven, and serious about making it to the next level. Among the players I am fortunate to have called a friend was Clarence Weatherspoon, who had a great career in the NBA, and Brett Favre, who went on to phenomenal success in the NFL, most famously for the Green Bay Packers. Being around Brett and other players who were headed for great things elevated my rim and reinforced the knowledge that my dreams were achievable.

Before long, the voices died down. Oh, they were still chattering away, maybe even shouting at times, but I didn't hear them anymore. All I could hear was about the life I was going to have, the life I could provide for my family, and the greater things that were going to become possible for me. I eventually got out of the negative part of my environment entirely.

Although I wasn't drafted out of college, I went to NBA basketball camp the summer after I finished school. I kept putting myself in environments with people who were trying to make it, not people who had given up and settled for less-difficult paths.

Making it to the NBA and standing on a court with Michael Jordan was an amazing opportunity for me, but I couldn't have gotten there if I hadn't identified my rim early and often, acknowledged it was there, and created a plan to rise above it. (More on plans in chapter 6.)

## Identifying Your Rims

### *Psychological Rims*

Basking in your comfort zone is the most deadly of all psychological rims. Your comfort zone can become your personal rim, and it happens in your head—between your ears. That's where you keep all your excuses and complaints, reasons why you didn't try or didn't become successful at something, and reasons you didn't achieve something or quit something. This internal monologue of misery and justification is the substance of your psychological rim.

Your personal rim has to do with psychological barriers fighting hard internally to keep you in your comfort zone, a place or situation in which you feel safe, at ease, and without stress. The problem here is that the road to success in anything usually leads out of your comfort zone. As the first really significant hurdle you have to clear, this rim couldn't be more critical to your success. To live your newly awakened dreams, you'll have to raise your psychological rim. What are the outer edges or the limits of your comfort zone? You've got to identify and understand them if you want to elevate your personal rims.

Excuses are a very poisonous psychological rim. "I didn't grow up in the correct environment" or "My father and mother weren't very nice" or "They didn't leave me this" are examples. If you let excuses establish a rim in your life, they will become self-fulfilling prophecies. Your piled-up failures become evidence that those things you *think* are the reasons you can't succeed *become* the reasons you can't succeed even though it didn't have to be that way. Your mind-set can rub off on your children and set them up for lives of mediocrity and discontent as well.

As you settle into a routine of your eight-to-five job, driving to work, taking out the trash, and shopping for shoes online, it's easy to stop dreaming of bigger and better things. After all, you're comfortable on a day-to-day basis. There's nothing wrong with that—unless you're aiming for a life above the rim. Nearly everything you'll need to do to reach your above-the-rim dreams will take place well outside your comfort zone.

I remember so many times when I've had to leave my comfort zone. During my second year in the NBA, I was with the Phoenix Suns and working hard to become known as a scorer off the bench. I wanted more playing time so I could prove what I could do. At that time, my teammate was Charles Barkley. He was an amazing teammate from whom I learned so much. He became a good friend, and we did everything together. As you can imagine, there was never a dull moment with Sir Charles. When I would get in the game, I would play opposite him and would get great cleanup plays because he drew all the attention as a superstar. Because of this, I got more playing time. Everything was great until this one game against the Houston Rockets. Eddie Johnson, a real good friend of mine, played for them; he was one of the all-time leading scorers in the league. The problem was that Eddie knew something no one else in the league knew—I couldn't go left. I had made it to the NBA, could put my head above the rim, shoot anywhere on the court, but I couldn't dribble with my left hand.

I'm in the game, the ball rotates to me, and the defender opens wide left, so wide it was like parting of the Red Sea. Any other athlete would have loved that, but I felt extremely uncomfortable. What I didn't realize was that Eddie had told his coach, "Courtney can't go left," and they baited my weakness. I took one dribble and passed the ball. It was obvious something was wrong. I was pulled out of the game and was so embarrassed. I had to do something about that.

The situation impacted me so much that I called my secret weapon, Tim Grover, the only one who could help me deal with something like that right away. He came up with a plan. At the All Star break, when all the players were resting, I flew to Chicago and basically tied my right hand behind my back for two weeks of practice.

CHAPTER FOUR

It paid off. A few weeks later, we played the Houston Rockets again, and it was payback time. I got in the game, and like clockwork, the ball came to me; they opened up wide to my left like the last time. You could see the smirk on the defender's face; he thought he had me figured out. I took two hard dribbles left, jumped with all my might, and dunked so hard that I almost broke the backboard! The looks on their faces were priceless.

After having achieved much in my life and after having gone through some failures as well, I know what I've practiced and what I'm writing about in this book are things you can use to excel and live above and beyond your rim.

But it all starts outside your comfort zone. Reading is outside some people's comfort zone. For others, dreaming might be outside their comfort zone. What's outside your comfort zone? If you want to be successful, you'll have to leave your comfort zone to achieve on a higher level. All great things happen outside your comfort zone. It's evident that our rims or glass ceiling has so much to do with the demographic structure of success

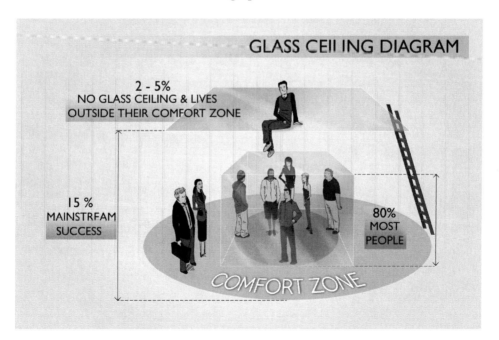

*GLASS CEILING DIAGRAM*

IDENTIFY YOUR RIMS

## Environmental Rims

Environmental rims are external; they can include your job, your neighborhood, and the negative people around you. An environmental rim could be as simple as a job that pays you $45,000 or $50,000 a year. Over time, that job becomes a rim when you base your self-worth on it. You've left behind the goals you had in high school or college of making $100,000, $200,000, or $1 million a year, and it all probably started with good intentions. You figured your current job was just a start; after all, no one starts at the top. But if you took the job without a goal and a plan, you likely got lost in the shuffle. After a few years, that salary is pretty ingrained as a rim and is holding you back.

Another environmental rim can be the negativity coming from the company you keep. Your relationships have a large bearing on the invisible barriers or limits placed on your life. Verbal negativity can come from your peers or even your family when you strive for goals that they aren't going for. You see this frequently when people express their ideas about starting a new business or becoming an actor or professional athlete—any goal that is tough and ambitious. I experienced that when I started to play basketball and expressed a desire to be in the NBA. It happened again after I retired from pro sports and expressed my desire to become an architect and design builder. When I told my agent about my plans, he asked, "Are you crazy?" Because I didn't buy his or anyone else's negative opinions, I became more financially prosperous than I had been in the NBA, and I felt just as fulfilled.

Sometimes, an environmental rim might be something that starts off positive, for instance, losing weight. If others start telling you, "It's okay to just have one. It's not like you're trying to compete in a fitness competition." If you're the only one in your social environment striving to be healthy, the little pushback comments about your little gut being "kind of cute" will have an effect. Over time, your standard drops, and you become comfortable being like everyone around you. Your clothes stop fitting, so you have to avoid places where you have to dress up or where people are more fit. This is experienced by most because the majority of people are trying constantly to seek comfort.

You reach only as high as your limits; if you want to go beyond your limits, live a life above and beyond your expectations, you have to be around people doing the same. You don't have to get away from people who are good to you and who mean a lot to you such as family and friends; it just means you should start spending time with people who think big, people whose actions are aligned with their big goals.

## Psychological Barriers Are Worse Than Environmental Barriers

Getting used to that low-paying job I mentioned above is an example of an environmental rim becoming a psychological barrier. Even though you may have originally considered the job a short-term solution, over time, being overworked and underpaid and not receiving recognition for your work will lower your confidence, making you feel you're not worth more.

The psychological barrier is far worse because it manifests itself internally, and that can cause more long-term damage. Your environment can get better, and you can change your environment, but if you're damaged internally, you can be living a silent war between your ears that can hold you back forever. Never take ownership of others' negative opinions or other external factors. You'll read how this can be personally devastating in the next chapter.

## Acknowledgment

Acknowledgement is a very important part of identifying your rim. You have to identify your strengths and your weaknesses. You have to acknowledge what your rims are, but you aren't likely to have the perspective you need especially when you're beginning this journey, so don't rely solely on your insights to identify and acknowledge your rims. Ask those close to you, including your spouse, friends, mentors, and coworkers, "What do you think my limits are? What do you think is my rim? What do you think I'm capable of?" It's amazing when you start hearing others' definitions of what your rims are and their take on your strengths and weaknesses.

Acknowledge what you've settled for. This is where you take a really hard, honest look at your life. Look at your goals, and use my action guide for success.

## Step One: Identify Your Psychological Rim and Comfort Zone

Identify those elements in your comfort zone that might be holding you back from achieving a higher level. Reflect on your dreams, goals, and desires of chapter 1 and write down the reasons you haven't achieved them or why you put them away. Ask yourself, *Where am I in those goals? What happened to those goals? What have I settled for?* This should make you uncomfortable. Once again, it's a comfort-zone thing, and we're going to get you out of it. That's okay. Embrace the uncomfortable; put everything on the table. You'll be opening a Pandora's box full of your dreams, but this Pandora's box is exciting and contains so many possibilities.

## Step Two: Contrast Step One with Where Your Life Is

Are you where you want to be? Make three columns on a piece of paper; label the first column "My desired outcome" and list your original goal, say, putting away $100,000. Label the second column "My current existence"; list your income and how much you've put aside toward your goal. List your expenditures outside you main bills that you don't have anything tangible to show for, such as dinners out, bar tabs, shopping, gym memberships that weren't used, and other such expenditures. Whatever your desired outcome deals with—a passion, fitness or a relationship—use the same model and input info where appropriate.

Label the last column "Excuses why I haven't reached my desired outcome," and write your excuses in it. This column is your rim. For example, in the above example, it could have been your plan to put away $100,000, but your excuses ended up being "I don't make enough money at my current job" or "Things keep coming up when I get extra money."

## Step Three: Define and Categorize Your Psychological vs. Environmental Rims

Separate your excuses in column three into categories. Category one should be psychological, those represented by your comfort zone, and these happen in your head. They can be emotional, thought-based suggestions that come to you when you ask yourself why you haven't reached your goal: *I don't know if I'm ready. I don't know if I'm good enough* are examples.

Your environmental rims are the exterior elements you blame. "I get off work late and don't have time to work out," "My wife is so negative about it; I don't think I can do it without her support," or "My job doesn't pay enough for me to save any." Whatever your environmental rims are, write them down and prepare for step four.

## Step Four: Wake-Up Call

Time to compare the two rims and identify reality vs. fabrication. Understanding why you haven't achieved your goal may shock you when you separate emotion from fact. Most people will be in denial about their rims. The reasons they have for not doing something are completely under their control. When you move past making excuses or blaming things that are actually under your control, you can make room for actual solutions. Once you write down those reasons, and there might be many, you've identified your "true" rims, but you'll notice that most are "not true" rims—they are generally fabricated and real only to you. Fortunately, because you'll break through them, they're real only for now.

Keep in mind, however, that some psychological and environmental rims are very real indeed; I'm thinking of clinical depression or bipolar disorder, or the mind-set of a child who grew up in poverty or a wife who has suffered abuse at the hands of her husband. Such true rims are limitations that must never be taken lightly. But doesn't mean that these situations are permanent; many successful people have overcome such true rims, but most rims are a result of choices and a lack of accountability for those choices.

Now that you understand the concept of your rim and have separated the different types, realize that they all can affect you if you take ownership of them. Your thoughts, good and bad, can determine your outcome

You'll find plenty of people willing to say that thoughts are not the same as reality, but thoughts can become reality. If I thought I couldn't have become an NBA player, I would never have tried, and my thinking would have become my reality. But I believed I could be an NBA player;

my actions followed my beliefs, and I worked hard to achieve my dream. I wasn't the greatest NBA player of my time, but I'll be very proud to be able to tell my son I made it.

## Exercise Drills to Define Your Rims—Questions to Ask Yourself

 What would you like to change about yourself that you've settled with?

 Why did you settle?

 Are you ready to make changes now? If not, why not?

 What about your career you've settled with would you like to change?

 Why did you settle with your career?

 Are you ready to make changes? If not, why not?

Are you comfortable around successful people? If not, why not?

Your answers to these questions are your rims. In the following chapters we will discuss how these rims evolved and how to break through any glass ceiling and elevate above any rim.

# CHAPTER

# EXPOSE THE THIEF

## *Don't Block Your Own Shots*

*If you sit in the shadow of your dreams, your future will be a dark place.*
—Chase Courtney

**W**E ARE ALL BORN WITH GREATNESS AND POWER. AS WE EVOLVE AND MAKE choices, the actions we take begin defining who we become and how we react to life. We can harness our power, and when used correctly and fueled with passion and desire, we can experience amazing results. But power not developed and used properly causes internal disaster. Without our knowing it, a different us starts to form and blend with our daily lives. It starts making our decisions and defining our thoughts.

The thief within is born. You start having conversations with an internal voice. You find yourself questioning everything, and your thoughts become negative. Over time, this builds; the thief begins stealing your happiness, relationships, and achievements.

In this chapter, we will expose the thief and hit the reset button on your life. Exposing the thief within is the most powerful principle of success in living life above the rim. Without exposing it, you can spend years searching, training, and developing but never achieve true success. This fact applies to people at every junction on their journeys, those just starting to recognize their rims as well as those who have reached a certain level of success and are trying to break through to a higher level. Exposing the thief is the most important thing you can do to break through your limitations and transform yourself.

What if you knew your life could change forever in an instant? What if someone uncovered something that was so dramatic, so prolific, and so profound that every thought process you'd have from that point on would be changed and the key to your success unlocked?

## The Thief Within

Imagine waking up one morning with the uneasy feeling that something wasn't right. You walk out of your bedroom and notice that some things have been moved around and others are plain missing. The house is definitely not how it was when you went to sleep. You'd go on high alert, sense your vulnerability, and ask yourself, *What's happening? Who did this?*

You'd check every door and window, but they're secure—no signs of forced entry. There's nothing you can do about the situation, but as you go on with your day, the intrusion weighs heavily on your mind. By evening, you're still cautious, concerned, and puzzled. As you're closing your eyes, you're thinking, *Did I leave the door unlocked? Did I do this? Did I do that?* Finally reassured everything is secure, you drift off to sleep.

The next morning, you open your eyes. The first thought you have is to check the house again. When you walk into the closet for a robe, you discover everything is gone! Dashing through the house, you see that your furniture and pictures have been moved around again. More things are missing around the house. Someone is stealing from you!

At wit's end, you dial 911. The police go through your home, take a statement, and check doors and windows, but once more, no sign of forced entry. Left with more questions than answers, you're feeling more vulnerable than ever. Who's coming into your home in the middle of the night and robbing you blind when you're there the whole time?

The police deliver some hard news. "It's obviously someone you know because there are no signs of forced entry; there are no signs of any damage anywhere. Do you have any enemies?" You tell them no one would wish you ill, but they still ask for a list of everyone you know, particularly those involved in personal or business relationships that have gone bad.

You decide to install a state-of-the-art security system, new locks on windows and doors, and video surveillance inside and out. At least you've taken steps to protect yourself, and you start feeling more secure. Your cameras will capture damning footage that'll put any criminal away.

CHAPTER FIVE

You go to bed still anxious but a bit reassured. You drift off to a fitful sleep and jump out of bed in the morning. It's painfully apparent the thief has been at work again. You dash to the video surveillance equipment to expose the thief. You see the person going through your things, moving some around and removing others entirely. One problem—the thief is you.

## The Thief and the "Monstars"

Just like everyone else, I have dealt with my own thief personally and professionally. My thief is very powerful but hidden. Have you ever planned to discuss a situation with someone and spent time before the meeting creating a story in your mind about the meeting? You converse with a voice in your head and create the outcome like writing a novel. We've all done that.

I experienced this when I was filming *Space Jam* with Michael Jordan. I played myself in the movie, but I also played a few of the villain characters called the "Monstars." We were filming the scene in the movie in which Jordan and the Looney Tunes were playing basketball against the villain to save Jordan from becoming an enslaved superstar left to sign autographs and to always lose against the people on the villain planet. The director had worked with other pro athletes and loved basketball. He always challenged athletes and played against them very aggressively. Usually, the athletes would succumb to his aggressive nature; they didn't want to get injured on set. Each time, the director would declare victory over the athlete and would brag about it.

Well, guess who was next on the director's list? You guessed it. He challenged me to a game of one-on-one on the set that happened to be painted green so the film could be edited to combine live actors and cartoon characters. I was going to pass on the offer until he asked, "What's wrong? You afraid to lose?" Oh no. He shouldn't have gone there! My athlete's blood started to stir. To make matters worse, Jordan said, "I'm betting on Courtney." I had to play the director. Jordan said to me, "Show him how the big boys do it." No backing out now. My first movie, and I'd have to embarrass the director in front of everyone. This wasn't looking good.

We started to play. At first, I was taking it easy until he made a few cheap shots. I turned it on. I made several shots, and he started getting reckless. I was going up for a dunk when he fouled me to stop the play, but it was too late—I was airborne, flying toward the basket when I felt contact and heard a crack. It was his nose! Bright-red blood went all over that bright-green set. I couldn't believe it. He was in pain. The crew cleared the set. I was instructed to go to our trailer.

I thought that I had finally got a shot at filming a movie, and what did I do? I broke the director's nose. My movie career was ending as fast as it had started. I was so disappointed. I started imagining different versions of negative outcomes. I imagined him saying, "Leave my set and don't ever come back!" Twenty very long minutes went by before I heard a knock. "Mr. Courtney, the director would like to see you immediately." My movie career was ending. I would be sent home in shame.

I walked onto the set and saw the director with a bloody towel on his face; crewmembers were helping stop his bleeding. He looked at me. You could hear a pin drop. "Joe Courtney, you've got a lot of heart. I want you in my next five movies!" The crew applauded, and the tension dissipated. The whole thing had turned out completely different from what my thief had led me to believe. If I had listened to that voice and gone back on set with a negative, defensive disposition, expecting a confrontation, my film experience in such a blockbuster film could have been stolen from me by my thief.

## The Birth of a Thief

Everyone has stolen from himself or herself at one point or another. Your inner thief may have stolen your relationships, your goals, or even your dreams. To be successful, you have to conquer the thief inside. Left unrestrained, it will sabotage every plan you make. No matter how great your dream is, no matter how organized your plan and your milestones are, your inner thief will find a way to drag you down. You must expose it for what it is, and then you can conquer it. But before you can expose your inner thief, you have to know where it came from.

The thief was born as a tiny seed in your childhood, probably when you were around four or so. It began with negative experiences ranging from minor disappointments to downright traumatic occurrences that congealed into learned behaviors and defenses. As time went on, you started to have automatic negative thoughts, knee-jerk thought patterns that evolve from certain experiences and behaviors.

Those who practice cognitive behavioral group therapy found in a study of the semantic content of automatic thoughts that the most common negative thoughts are related to the fear of poor social performance, negative labels, opinions of others, or the anticipation of negative outcomes in feared situations. These automatic thoughts stem from three underlying themes: experiencing anxiety, negative self-evaluation, and fear of negative evaluation.

You developed a defense against any pain. If your parents argued over money and ended up divorced, you would be prone to develop a defense against this by becoming a hard worker and developing a love-hate relationship with money. As you got older, this would have reconfirmed itself, and you would've ended up facing a psychological block every time you got close to more success or more money.

Even positive experiences can contribute to subconscious behaviors that undermine your success. Every time a new circumstance triggers your "thief" behaviors, they become more thoroughly entrenched. These negative experiences have more consequences than most people realize.

## How Negative Childhood Experiences Affect You as an Adult

The experiences and environments surrounding a growing child play key roles in that child's adult life. Children growing up in unstable environments or suffering abuse do not experience proper brain development. These environments tend to lead to behavioral issues that generally result in unhealthy adult lifestyles of addictions to alcohol, smoking, drugs, or obesity.

Obesity and smoking are two common problems adults face today and are often linked. Many eat or smoke to cope with emotions, often negative ones that arise from unhappy childhoods involving physical abuse or molestation. Those dealing with obesity experience lack of self-esteem, blame themselves for their extra weight, and often suffer from depression. Smoking is also linked to those negative effects. Those who decide to quit smoking generally gain a large amount of weight because they lose their coping mechanism and turn to food as an alternative. Obesity can lead to low self-esteem and depression, which can affect professional life and decisions.

Those who suffer from low self-esteem often have difficult times finding good careers. They assume their abilities are inadequate for a decent career they settle for jobs below their qualifications, making it difficult for them to make any significant achievements. Companies are less likely to hire those who clearly lack confidence in themselves; how could someone lacking self-confidence succeed? Self-esteem plays a huge role in professional life and the ability to achieve higher goals.

Negative childhood experiences can include being bullied, abused, or malnourished, and the effects of such experiences can last a lifetime. If a child's body does not receive adequate nutrition, it resorts to breaking down proteins for energy that are necessary for telling the body when to eat and how much food should be consumed. If these proteins are never replenished, the body stays in a constant state of starvation regardless of how much food is consumed; the body remains hungry.

When malnourished children grow up and have food readily available as an adult, their tendency is to eat as much as they can, and if that food is highly processed, they won't get needed nutrients and protein. They eat and eat, trying to satiate themselves but never quite achieving fullness. The result? Obesity.

It's a common misconception that children are resilient and will forget any negative experiences from childhood as they grow older. It's been shown that many problems arising in adults are based on childhood experiences. Children are resilient, but their brains and bodies retain early impressions that can affect their lives, good, bad, or otherwise, as adults.

As you age, the thief develops; it thrives on your failures. When you didn't make the cut for the cheerleading team, the thief told you it knew that would happen. When you failed a chemistry final, it said you were stupid. When your girlfriend dumped you for a guy with better body, the thief said that you'd never find love. When you were passed over for a promotion, the thief said that you'd never get ahead, that no one was ever going to give you a chance.

Eventually, this devastating mental poison becomes a part of who you are. The thief is like some kind of evil twin inside you; its thoughts are intertwined with yours. It's everywhere you go.

Left unchecked, the thief becomes more powerful and ends up making all your decisions for you. You're no longer your own person. Every time you get out of your comfort zone, it does whatever is necessary to push you back into it. Your dreams end up buried under a pile of negativity and disappointment. Eventually, he starts operating in plain sight. It's no longer a collection of misguided defense mechanisms designed to protect you; it becomes someone out to protect itself; it doesn't care what happens to you.

## Eject the Thief from Your Game

The thief has a great life in your existence, in your being, and it loves being undetected. It manipulates all the decisions you make. It shows itself in conversations. When someone tells you about some exciting thing that happened to him or her, your thief will ask you, *Did that really happen? It sounds too good to be true, doesn't it? Maybe you should see if you can catch that person in a lie.* This all happens in an instant.

The average person has more than ten thousand thoughts per day. That's a lot of thinking! But consider this: over 90 percent of those thoughts are negative. If positive thinking gets just 10 percent of your attention, the thief is running and ruining your life.

But don't panic. You're going to expose your thief and send it to the bench. Scratch that. You're going to eject it from the game. Once you expose the thief, your life can change dramatically. Once you know it's there, you can begin to regain control of your life and your future. Be warned, though; the thief never really goes away; it can only be controlled. That ugly, hateful, little voice is always ready to pop up and rain on your parade the minute you cease to be vigilant about keeping it under control. In the best-selling book *Little Voice Mastery*, Blair Singer referred to that self-sabotaging behavior and self-talk as the "little voice" in your head.

Understand that the thief exists and is powerful. Understand also that once you control the thief, *you* can be powerful and achieve your goals—from relationships to success and whatever else you want in life.

## Steps to Expose Your Thief Within

- Identify your strong suits, your social survival attributes—for instance, work ethic, protector instincts, and ability to be in control.

- Identify the opposing side of these strengths and reflect on your past to find when and where you were exposed to them and experienced negativity because of them. If your strength is helping others, you might have experienced pain in the past by being bullied.

- Identify your negative thoughts—the internal ones and those that come from outside, perhaps from others.

- Probe your past for the first sign of internal or external negativity.

- Take away the power of your negative story. Write down what happened and read it aloud often enough that you start becoming numb to it.

This has become your story. You've been telling yourself subconsciously that you have to be extreme one way or another because of something painful that happened to you. Realize you took ownership of it and buried it deep inside. However, it's now out, and you're no longer its victim. Repeatedly reading it aloud will take away the power it has over you. It will become less impactful until it's finally just words.

If this is starting to hit home to you, perform these steps now. The process is organic; you want to deal with it while the situation is unearthed through reading this or you may rebury it.

CHAPTER FIVE

## Deprogram Your Inner Thief

Get used to the idea you've been programmed. Since childhood, you've been getting programs of information and experiences that serve as an underlying code, a fixed way of being that exists in your language, thinking, and behavior—some of it good, some of it not so good.

The experience of watching your parents argue over money may have caused you to look at money in a negative way or drove you to make as much money as possible. If someone called you fat, that may have driven you to extreme workouts or it may have devolved into a circle of unhealthy eating and self-loathing. Whatever your negative experiences were, they had a dramatic impact on whom you became. During your formative years, these negative experiences caused a reaction in your mind not too different from the way your body reacts to a germ or other pathogen. Just as you develop antibodies to defend against pathogens, you developed defensive systems to protect yourself from negative experiences early on.

Regardless of what your bad experiences were, the response that sprang forth and carried you into adulthood is essentially a defense mechanism to protect you from bad experiences. Being aware that the thief exists and acknowledging where it shows up is the first step to start diffusing and dealing with it. You become aware of the initial effects when identifying your environmental rim we discussed in principle 4. These influences have been taking place most of your life, and they are also apparent in your present. You just have to realize they are there. Once you're aware, a shift can happen internally; you can change directions and start distinguishing between what's real from the manipulations of your inner thief.

For example, when someone you've had an argument with in the past is telling you something, your thief might remind you of that disagreement and put negative thoughts in your mind about that person. You might respond to that person in a negative or condescending manner without realizing it. Your thief is trying to validate something that may not be true anymore, resulting in unnecessary friction between you and that person.

To combat this, you have to be conscious of it and take control of your space by deciding to be positive no matter what. This will give you a sense of control and allow you to not assume that the situation will end up negative.

This can start halting the process of your being responsible for your part of damaging relationships and help you develop a proactive offense against your inner thief. But be careful—your inner thief can be very manipulative, and even though you find out that it exists, it can still secure its place inside you by making you think it's trying to protect you.

## Offense vs. Defense

Be aware of the difference between your inner thief manipulating you to defend against negativity by overcompensation versus actually developing a proactive offense against negative influences. When it comes from the thief, it's derived through negativity. When it comes from a proactive offense, above the rim, it's fueled by positivity and comes from a place of bettering yourself and your environment.

When the thief drives you to develop a defense, you can overcompensate by becoming strong in certain areas. Running from the memory of being called lazy way back when can drive you to be a high achiever who never sits still or wastes time for too long. But as you're creating a defense against this negative experience, you are also developing strong negativity against these sources. How do you know this? Well, the fact that you're reacting to negative voices in your head is a pretty big clue.

## Don't Let the Thief Fool You

The thief within can fool you into believing that overcompensation is a kind of reward you get from negative responses. If someone calls you a name, you immediately have negative thoughts. Of course, that part seems normal because those instances involve very rude behavior, but even in situations without overt confrontation, you may start to have negative thoughts. Perhaps you have negative thoughts when you see someone who is at a healthy weight or someone who's thin.

So what do we gain for these negative thoughts? What are the instant gratifications for your defense? One of them is to make you right. Remember, you're in protection mode, so when you encounter negative triggers such as comments or behaviors that incite your defenses, you immediately contradict them either mentally or aloud. You're right and they're wrong. Being right prevents you from feeling dominated; it gives you a sense of control. It also allows you to justify yourself, and in the process, you can devalue others. In your mind, you just won, so you avoid losing, which seems a lot to gain from your negative response.

Do you see the problem here? It's just wrong and a poor way to communicate. Even though successful people can convert negatives into positives because of their confidence, self-awareness, and uncanny knack of staying focused on their goals, for most people, it's a poisonous concoction brewing that will leave holes in their lives. Some may think developing a strong side in any way necessary is a great idea. Well, yes, in one sense, it can create a strong side of you. Some people call it your strong suit. But the problem with this is your defense starts costing you. You get boxed in to a thought process and eliminate options that could be very rewarding.

This "strong suit" offense can also dominate your personality. You become strong in one area but lack severely in others. If you're all about one thing, you'll be out of balance. If your strong suit is extreme fitness, you can sometimes be so extreme that you can't enjoy yourself.

I overcompensated from an aspect of my own thief. When I was younger, my father was always very negative and spoke only to ridicule or criticize when things didn't go right; he never said anything positive when things went well. He constantly told me I wouldn't amount to anything. Even though I was a high-achieving artist and had been accepted into a special school for the arts, the fact I didn't play sports then was a big problem for him. It haunted me because I felt I was different but didn't know why.

On the other hand, my mother would tell me, "You can be anything you want in life," and she supported all my efforts the best she could. Defining my identity was a constant internal struggle for me. The positive reinforcement I received from my mother when we watched the Bulls play that day won me over to basketball. (Jordan still doesn't know he was the reason I started playing basketball). Every time I got tired and thought about quitting training for the day, I heard my father say, "You're never going to be anything." That would make me angry and would make me push myself even harder. I started running from that voice and doing anything I could to prove he was wrong about me. It created two of my strong suits: working hard and never giving up.

I had positive and negative influences working at the same time. If my future would have been connected to just one or the other as a source for me to pull from to reach my goal, I wouldn't have gotten as far. I chose to focus on my inner passion and belief in myself—that fueled my successes in life.

Unfortunately, the offense and defense the thief can create often get out of control and become a new problem. Just like the potentially deadly allergic reactions your body can develop in a misguided attempt to protect you from a perceived pathogen, these defense mechanisms can rob you of happiness and success.

Because I was so driven and haunted by the fear I would fail, I overworked constantly. I recall trainer Tim Grover telling me to take the time off after the season so I'd be fresh when I started training again. Afraid I would somehow lose a step, get out of shape, or worse, "not amount to anything," I ran day and night and continued pushing even though everyone else was resting and it would have been okay for me to do the same. The thief was at work, and though some may see the strong suit it created as a positive, it can rob you of precious aspects of your life. Without proper balance, you will pay a high price because the effects can be detrimental. I became a workaholic who never relaxed enough to enjoy the simple things in life. This became even more noticeable when I got married and had a child. My wife told me so many times, "Joe, just relax and let it go," but I would work through countless holidays. I was building my construction company, positioning it to be one of the top companies not only in my area but in the whole United States. I wanted to grow and make more money, so I worked seven days a week, and contractors were at my door 24/7. Lee stopped me one day. "Joe, why are you working so hard? I know you said you're doing this for us, but what good is all the money if we don't have you? We just want you."

I realized then that my thief was out of control. I had a big house, multiple properties, nice cars, a thriving business, and a beautiful wife and child, but inside, I battled a constant feeling of being unfulfilled. I was driving for success to prove my father wrong. I hadn't been allowing myself to enjoy the fruits of my labor, which left a void, a feeling of unfulfillment.

My moment of change came when I exposed my own thief. I acknowledged that my behavior stemmed from negativity in my past. I took the steps mentioned at the end of this chapter and put my thief to rest. Even though it still shows its ugly head from time to time, I found a balance. What I'm doing now is trying to prevent others from letting their strong suits steal other parts of their lives and help them gain well-balanced happiness and success.

## The High Cost of Robbing Yourself

The thief steals from every aspect of your life and personality, and you may not have noticed some of its thievery. Think about the many different ways you're robbing yourself of a better life by letting the thief run loose, and use those as part of your motivation to overcome it. The thief steals your:

### Vitality and Well-Being

Even if you're into extreme fitness as a result of the thief, you could be living a life that's out of balance. Well-being comes from living a balanced, complete life.

### Self-Expression

The thief prevents you from being open with those around you about how you feel and also prevents you from being open to new ideas and experiences.

## Love and Relationships

When you're trapped inside your comfort zone, you lose the ability to have intense love and passion. You simply cannot connect with another on a truly intimate level. Even your nonromantic relationships wither because of the way the thief shapes your interactions with them.

Because of all the things the thief has taken, you're likely to experience:

## Unhappiness

You're less likely to hear it in your own voice, but have you ever talked to someone who has a negative tone? They just seem unhappy; no matter what happens, they find ways to be negative about it. Such negativity comes as a result of the things they're losing to the thief. Listen carefully to yourself to see if you can hear it in your voice.

## Procrastination

Getting caught up listening to the ugly voices in your head—voices that come from the thief—will tend to put you in neutral. You will procrastinate, unable to move forward.

## Being Unfulfilled

Do you ever feel that nothing is ever enough? No matter what the circumstance, you're somehow always left feeling unfulfilled.

## Being Argumentative

Instead of talking situations through calmly, you feel defensive and try to "win" conversations at all costs. In the back of your mind, the thief is trying to steal the discussion by flooding your system with negative thoughts.

## Being Negative

The glass is always half empty. The thief simply won't allow you the optimism to see what's going right in your world. You always focus on the things that aren't working out.

### Quitting Easily

No matter what you start, you always quit.

These things happen hundreds of times a day. Over time, they become so ingrained that you don't recognize them, and you start developing extreme coping mechanisms. You could end up coping with the thief with:

### Abusing Alcohol or Other Substances

When you feel frustrated, unhappy, loveless, and unfulfilled, it's easy to make the mistake of thinking alcohol or other drugs will make you feel better.

### Being Verbally Abusive

When you're frustrated at every turn, you become more and more likely to blow up at the people in your life who care about you, including your spouse and children or even innocent bystanders in the grocery store.

### Being Physically Abusive

Enough said. If you find yourself coping with your frustrations by physically harming others, get help immediately—today. If you're in a relationship with someone who is hurting you for whatever reason, get out now.

### Being Self-Destructive

For some reason, every time you get close to the next big moment, the next big milestone, you find a way to undermine yourself. You set up your own downfall and prevent yourself from achieving.

The sum of all these is one thing: the thief that was designed to protect you at its inception is now in control and no longer looking out for you. When people who act as positive influences try to help you achieve or introduce new things that could change your life for the better, the thief comes in and completely collapses on them. It's fighting for its very existence; it's deeply entrenched, a part of you. And right now, it's in control.

## Take Back Control

Controlling the thief means getting back your real life, not just a corner that you were sitting in, what you thought was your real life for all these years—no. I mean a full-fledged, whole life. Instead of being unhappy, you'll have happiness. Instead of procrastinating, you'll be on top of your game, conquering challenges every time you get the opportunity. Instead of being unfulfilled, you'll be fulfilled. Can you imagine?

Instead of being argumentative, you will be lovable, compassionate, and fair. You'll be able to have an opinion and still have peace. Instead of looking at life as a glass half empty, you will look at it as half full. You will say, "Oh my God, look at the opportunity that exists in every situation!" And you will quit quitting. Can you imagine having a life with no quitting? Someone once said, "If you're tired of starting over, stop quitting."

Think about how your life would change if you woke up tomorrow without the limitations imposed on you by the thief. Think about how your goals would change. Think about how your future would change.

You can be happy and positive, on time, proactive, and fulfilled by everything you do. You can feel compassionate and get along with others. You can look at life as a glass half full. Most important, you'll never feel like quitting. These are the results of exposing the thief, and these results can begin as soon as you choose to make them happen. Exposing the thief is a game changer.

## Proactive Offense to Control Your Thief

- Acknowledge that your thief exists.

- Write down everything you're thankful for.

- Declare and define a new vision of your life. Refer to principles 1 and 2 to assist you with this.

- Get rid of negative words such as *can't*, *won't*, and *hate*, and switch to power positives such as *can*, *will*, and *love*. Your words have power that your subconscious absorbs.

- Choose to be proactive. Take control now. When you start thinking negative thoughts, take a positive action to combat them. If you think you can't do something, act immediately and give it your best. If you're in sales and think a customer doesn't want what you have, call that customer immediately to introduce your product. (More about taking action in an upcoming chapter.)

- Own your space by taking 100 percent responsibility for your actions and statements, and choose to be positive in all interactions.

- Don't assume anything. Be results-based in your thoughts and actions. Let confirmation replace assumption.

- Reprogram by overwriting negativity with positivity daily. Read self-help books or listen to motivational material. My *Life above and beyond the Rim* audio series is a good start. More info about this at the end of this book.

- Do something positive toward your desired outcome daily.

Now you understand how to recognize the thief, where it comes from, and how it evolves. You've learned how to keep it under control, and you understand the manipulative gratification it offers and the extreme coping mechanisms you have formed because of it.

## Remove the Power from the Thief

Now it's time to come clean. To move on, you have to become unblocked, but you must first forgive yourself and the person who caused your pain. Write down and explain what happened; be as detailed as memory allows. Make sure to include how it made you feel. *(This feeling has become your belief of how you see yourself)*. At the end, write that you no longer blame that person for what happened and that you forgive him or her. Read it aloud.

Read it out loud repeatedly. This depowers the experience by decreasing its impact on you each time you repeat it. You will find after a while you become numb to it. If you find yourself not having full closure with your experience, you may need to have a conversation with whomever was involved to achieve that. If the person is not around, imagine he or she is sitting in front of you, read your written experience, and express your feelings. I did this with my father, and it gave me a feeling of permanent closure. I caution you in taking this measure, though; remember that your happiness resides within you and not the other person. The value of the results you attain is not in the other person's response, but in the choice you're making not to let that response have control of you. If you decide to reach out to the person at the source of your discomfort, you have to do so coming from the right place. Remember that the thief will try to manipulate you into trying to be "right" when you have such a conversation, so remember that you're not making this call to be right or to prove someone else wrong—you're making it to gain control and own your space and right to be positive and pure to yourself no matter what the response from the other party is. Others may respond negatively, but remember that they have their own thieves they don't know exist and aren't taking ownership of their responses. If you have a physically abusive relationship with this person, do not do this. Otherwise, make the call, read your written experience to them, and express your forgiveness. Let them know how excited you are for the potential of the rest of your life.

When you complete this process, a sense of power will come over you, and this feeling will gain momentum. You should begin having improved confidence, a better self-image, and more control over your emotions.

By exposing the thief, you will change the direction of your life, your choices, and your possibilities. Understand that your inner thief will not go away overnight but will become more silent over time. Knowing that the thief exists is a huge step, but you must apply the knowledge you gain to win against your thief.

I suggest that you periodically review the exercises in this chapter and use them to improve your journey toward success. Take some time to reflect, but also take some time to imagine. Now that you've exposed

CHAPTER FIVE

the thief, it's time to imagine and create the new possibilities for your life. After you have completed this, you'll be ready to start living your life above the rim. The following chapters will help you complete the process. You will be victorious!

## Exposing the Thief Transformation Drills

No transformation—personally or environmentally—can happen without exposing the thief. Take a look at your life. Take a look at your thief. Using the tools mentioned in this chapter, go through the following exercises and send your life in a positive, new direction.

 Write down the negative thoughts you have that are immediately apparent after reading this chapter and look for a consistent pattern in them. We have thousands of thoughts per day, and most are negative, so you should have no problem coming up with a list.

 If they deal with a person or group, uncover the source of the negativity by recalling the first instant you remember having a negative experience with that person or group.

 Write down the negative thoughts you have about yourself, and repeat the previous step, but this time, uncover when you first started having these thoughts.

Take a look at your experiences before you move on to the next chapter. Think about what has happened in your life going back to your early childhood, when you were between three and six. Try to identify a situation that caused you pain or made you extremely uncomfortable. It might not come to you right away, but keep at it. Was there someone who said something to you that matches the negativity you wrote down in the previous step?

 Having trouble putting your finger on anything? Identify what makes you positive and strong right now, your good habits and your strong suits. Those strong suits have an opposing effect; you could have been teased as a child for being overweight, which caused you to overcompensate by being fanatical about fitness. Your parents' divorce may have caused you to think you weren't accepted, so you developed a strong suit of being overly generous to ensure people like you. Identify what happened that caused you to create your strong suits. That will prepare you to expose the thief because you will understand the catalysts, the traumatic experiences that change your makeup.

# CHAPTER

6

# ROAD MAP TO YOUR DREAMS

## Write Your Success Playbook

*Victorious warriors win first and then go to war, while*
*defeated warriors go to war first and then seek to win.*
—Sun Tzu, *The Art of War*

UNDERSTANDING YOUR RIM IS THE FIRST STEP, BUT CREATING A PLAN TO elevate above your rim is the step where the rubber meets the road. If you don't have a path to your destination, how could you get there? A few things are fun to look at while you're spinning in a circle, but your life is not one.

High achievers create success plans, powerful tools to reach goals. Champions in business, sports, and life in general understand that without a success plan, they're leaving too much to chance. Your success plan or success playbook becomes your system. When I played with the Bulls, this was very evident. The team was a well-oiled machine. Coach Phil Jackson and his staff implemented a plan for success that got rid of the distracting minutiae so we could focus on what was important and use a hundred percent of our energy on what counted. Jackson says, "The road to freedom is a beautiful system."

We'd run the triangle offense, and the results were beautiful. It raised our level of confidence in ourselves and in each other, and it created unity in our system. Everyone knew where they had to be at all times. Each player had a role, and because we didn't waste energy on what didn't matter, we could put all our efforts into mastering our roles. In an interview in 2013, Jackson said, "What attracted me to the triangle was the way it empowers the players, offering each one a vital role to play as well as a high level of creativity within a clear, well-defined structure." The results were victories and repeated championships. Jackson's success system has resulted in eleven titles for his teams and has made him one of the greatest coaches in history. Creating a success plan is understated, often overlooked, and not taken seriously by people who constantly fail. It's so important for several reasons. First, it maps out an efficient path to any goal; the fastest way between two points is a straight line. Creating a success blueprint will give you a clear-cut path to your destination and will represent that straight line to your goal. A solid plan will get you through the unexpected dips in the road. Things will knock you off your path at times, but if you know where you're going and how to get there, you can always get back on track.

Second, with an accurate plan of action, you can level the playing field; you can overcome shortcomings in talent or skill. I had a late start; I started basketball at the end of my freshman year in high school. Even though I was talented, I had shortcomings I had to overcome. I wrote out a plan to work on my skills after school and fit in extra work to refine my skills. I read books and studied top-performing athletes relentlessly. I caught up quickly, and my talent took over.

Later in high school and in college, I got by pretty well because of the plan I had put in place to correct my deficiencies and boost my talent. But when I started making my push for the NBA, I noticed that things were different, that talent wasn't enough. I went to NBA Summer Leagues and started competing against the best players from around the country, including NBA players. They were all talented. Even though I had a plan to get there initially, I had to really sharpen my pencil because the margin for error became little if none at all. I reviewed my plan and wrote out adjustments to it. I repeated the steps from my original plan but at a much higher level. I followed it to a T. I started getting advice from personal trainers for peak fitness and coaches for game strategies. I ended up creating my own opportunities because I was so prepared, and I even surpassed players who were more talented and were even drafted. My plan worked!

Third, a plan keeps you honest on your progress. It can provide checks and balances so you know where you are whether good or bad. You'll often feel you're working so hard toward a goal and think you're so much further ahead than you really are. Sometimes, it's due to the emotion of the change you're experiencing at the beginning of your success plan, which done correctly should keep you out of your comfort zone. You might jump on the scale after a week of working out and eating right, expecting to see that you're down ten pounds. Finding out you're down only three will sober you up. This is a time when a lot of people veer off, but if you had a plan that clearly defined your milestones, you would stick to your plan. After three or four more weeks, your metabolism would kick in and you'd start burning fat in your sleep. You'd end up losing eighteen pounds! This attitude becomes even more important when your goals may take three to five years to attain.

Plan creation has been used for thousands of years. Can you imagine building the pyramids without one or going to battle for our country but just winging it? The Battle of Yorktown comes to mind in this regard; proper planning and commitment to the plan resulted in an enormous victory despite a huge imbalance of power between the British and the Americans. When the first shots were fired in Lexington and Concord in 1775, it seemed laughable to the British that George Washington's group of poorly armed, loosely organized colonists had the audacity to challenge the massive, experienced British military. The rebels' chances of success seemed even more remote when the American colonies formally declared their independence from Great Britain on July 4, 1776.

The Americans would have been outmatched significantly in any head-to-head battle, but Washington knew he simply had to avoid the British defeating him. He knew if he could keep his army in the field and the British at battle long enough, the newly declared republic would survive. The longer the war lasted, the greater the odds were that the British would eventually be dragged into other wars that would threaten their country and they would tire. The plan was executed. On October 17, 1781, Cornwallis asked for a cease fire, and he surrendered two days later. The plan had worked. Not long after, the British government collapsed over embarrassment over the defeat at Yorktown. The new officials authorized a treaty on September 3, 1783, that acknowledged the independence of the United States.

## Create Your Passion Playbook

Achieving your dreams begins with visualizing them, and a Passion Playbook is a great way to visualize your dreams. Creating a Passion Playbook gives you something concrete to look at and touch. Creating a tangible manifestation of your dreams is important. It's easy to think about your dreams when you're in your favorite recliner and you haven't had to face the realities of many obstacles. But later on, when you're having a rotten day or week or month, you'll need something to hold on to, a physical reminder of what you're working toward. Your Passion Playbook will give you the push you need to break through each barrier and continue to rise above the rim.

## Purposes for a Passion Playbook

- to remind you why you're working toward a goal

- to identify and clearly define your vision

- to reinforce your daily affirmations

- to serve as an emotional and physical manifestation tool

- to subconsciously connect you with your outcome

To make your Passion Playbook, select a medium. You can glue magazine cutouts on poster board, or you can create one on a computer; this will allow you to share your Passion Playbook with people on Facebook and other social media. These people can root for you. Programs such as Pinterest allow you to create and attach different photographs, images, and texts related to your dream that you can share.

Once you've got a platform from which to work, start adding representations of the things you want out of life. Don't think about money at this point, and don't worry about how far-fetched the things you want seem right now. Just think about what you want out of life. Your Passion Playbook can have anything and everything on it—an improved relationship or your search for love. You can add a picture of your new spouse or just two people in love. A lot of the things you add will be representations of an improved lifestyle. Maybe you want financial freedom, a new house, a nice vacation, or valuable time with your loved ones.

With the list of things you want in mind, find representations of them on the Internet and add them to your board. Talk to others to help you zero in on what you want. If one thing on your board is travel, discuss with a travel agent some of the places you want to visit. As your dream develops, what used to be a blank board will start to bloom into a fleshed-out vision of who you want to be and where you want to be. One unexpected benefits of creating a Passion Playbook is the additional inspiration you will get and how you'll better understand your dreams.

## Writing Your Plan

Once your Passion Playbook is complete, start writing to document your plan; unwritten plans are just a bunch of statements and wishes. This is a reason so many people never stick with their New Year's resolutions; 25 percent abandon them within a week, and over 60 percent quit within six months. Writing your plan forces you to clarify what you want and identify facts and details; it will also motivate you to focus your energy on action and help you overcome any initial resistance you feel to starting. It's particularly important to write down financial plans. In the long term, a few dollars saved here and there can really add up. Your short-term goals are just as important because they form your habits that produce your long-term results.

Your written plan could help you define your target audience, marketing plan, expenses, and more. Writing your plan makes it real for you, but you will have to uncover specifics about your field to do so properly. Here are a few tips to help you get started.

## Tips for Writing Your Plan

- **Get an organizer for your success plan.** Because we process so much information daily, don't just add your new plan to your current system of organizing; you'll get distracted by all the other things in it. Get a separate organizer for your plan—nothing goes in it but your dream. This will keep you focused and accountable.

- **Write down what you plan to achieve.** Successful people will say you have to know where you're going to get there; a documented dream has a higher probability of success. Actually write down your dream, frame it, and hang it where you'll see it. Something magical happens when you write things down—they become a commitment, something you own. Each time I went for something great in my life, I wrote down what I wanted to achieve in bite-sized goals. Making it to the NBA was a huge undertaking on the surface and included training to get in shape, improving shooting, rebounding, defense, jumping ability, quickness, and more. I wrote down the main goal and each moving part, and I created a mini-plan for each to keep me on track and inform my subconscious mind.

  The writing process will create exciting and fruitful things; it will ignite new ideas about how to improve your progress and performance. Make sure you document them when they come up. Because your plan can evolve, you may have to work on it weekly until it is complete. This process will require short-term and long-term goal setting and will push you out of your comfort zone, but the results will be more than worth it.

- **Write down your vehicle to achieve your dream.** Whether your goal is financial, starting your own business, or becoming a top performer in your industry, you must choose what method will help you reach your goal. If it's starting a new business, choose something you're passionate about but that also has the capacity to generate the money you need to reach your goal. Seek advice from those involved in your dream endeavor. Assess your passion and skill sets so you're not tempted to stray outside those areas or you may end up going down the wrong road.

You can find financial freedom if you combine your passion with the knowledge base you've already acquired. Though this may be only a start and you will need additional work, training, and experience to achieve success on a higher level, you will at least have the correct building blocks and foundation. Once you've found what you're looking for, visualize what success in your business would look like and document it.

- **Create a success calendar and document your desired success date.** Writing the date you want to achieve your goal by is a powerful motivator. You not only start the clock to your success and create urgency, you also make it visual and measurable. You can accurately calculate the time, work backward, and create a daily schedule of actions, a timeline, and the results you expect. Use index cards to start your process of creating a DMO, a daily method of operation. You can use your daily organizer or create a custom one that has information only about your desired outcome.

- **Use index cards to track your progress.** Index cards are easy to use, and they have two sides. They will allow you to see your progress and help it sink in. If you're trying to lose weight, for example, writing your weight-loss goals down will make you accountable; you'll think twice before getting the fries and shake with your order.

- **Use a dry-erase board.** I strongly believe in this one. Whenever I'm plotting my way to a goal, I keep track of my daily status on my dry-erase board. It's easy to change info, and you can use different colors to identify pluses and minuses. The one in my office is a valuable tool to keep me on track and let me know where I am daily.

- **Allow alone time to review your progress.** There's nothing worse than distractions when you have your game face on. Give yourself adequate alone time to review and absorb your plan. Read your plan outline every day, and review your progress. But this time should be for you only!

## Create a Time Frame

Even a well-thought-out plan is meaningless without some kind of clock. By integrating a time frame in your plan, you will give yourself structure and go one more step in combating inertia. Be aggressive but realistic as you set a date for completion. You'll want to realize your dream in your lifetime, but expecting to fulfill all your goals in six months will most likely set you up for disappointment.

As you're establishing a time frame, don't get bogged down in any "drop-dead" date. All you're doing right now is creating a guide; you're imposing some structure on your dreams. If you don't hit your deadline, don't worry; take what you've learned and readjust the clock to better suit your situation.

Many people set goals with no timelines; the goal becomes a moving target that goes from six months to a year to five years and then to never. Embracing definite times and dates will make your dreams real. Definitely set a time and date to achieve your goal, but don't worry if you don't hit it. If you discover you've come 60 percent of the way to your goal, you're 60 percent further than you would have been if you hadn't started working.

Reaching your goal is more important than doing so on a timeline, but your schedule will give you an orderly process for reaching it. By embracing the time and date, you give yourself an opportunity and a chance to be accountable, which will turn into your achieving success in a big way.

## Create a Milestone Blueprint

Milestones are the shorter-term goals that help you reach your long-term goal. Setting up a timeline that includes dates for completion of these smaller goals will help keep you on track for the larger goal. If your long-term goal requires you to finish your degree, set milestones to apply to three universities by a certain time, complete your financial aid paperwork by another specific date, and earn your degree by a certain (albeit significantly longer) time frame. If your goal is real estate, set a date for getting the study materials for the real estate license test, a date for registering for the test, and a date for getting your real estate license.

I made milestones for myself when I was trying to make it into pro sports. I told myself that by a certain time, I wanted to be at a certain location. I wanted to go to college, so I set the deadlines I needed to accomplish that.

Simple milestones can make a big difference. When I started running to get in better shape, I didn't have a lot of time, so I ran at night. I turned the negative of insomnia into a positive. I was getting in better shape; I hit my milestones, and I slept better. Amazing!

Chart your progress based on your milestones, which can be daily, weekly, or monthly goals you're accountable to. This will let you to see how you're doing between milestones.

A daily method of operation can keep you on track, and it's a really good feeling when you achieve a milestones. A consultant might set a goal of gaining a certain number of new clients in thirty days. That consultant will establish a daily method of operation that will allow him or her to achieve weekly milestones and ultimately the monthly milestone by contacting prospective clients, maybe twenty a week, and turning a quarter of them into actual clients. Four weeks? Twenty new clients. Even if this accountant falls short and gains only ten clients in that month, that's still plenty more than zero. Charting your progress is very important in the process of accountability.

You'll want to set up a structure, and that can be accomplished by utilizing all the tools I've mentioned. They certainly can utilize technology, but the point is to come up with a structure with accountability. Technology can be a hindrance if it's distracting, and it can sometimes take you off track. But using technology in the correct format can actually help you develop an accountability system that will remind you when you forget.

When I'm coaching leaders in my *Life above and beyond the Rim* success transformation system, I have them set an alarm with details about their overall goals and specific points of achievement as well—the milestones I've mentioned. A big milestone could be a goal at the end of the month that's measured by three weekly, smaller milestones they check in on. Our daily method of operation consists of setting alarms in our phones to give us reminders of what we need to do that day.

Today's technology—iPhones, droids, and others—can make your life so much easier, but first develop your processes, goals, and milestones on paper to make them visual, verbal, and tangible as we discussed earlier. You really want your milestones to be etched into your mind, and technology can help you do that.

To be accountable, focus on time and date. Some people have differences of opinions on time and date; many success coaches will tell you to be outcome-oriented, which I truly believe in. But in a system with built-in accountability in terms of times and dates, your milestones will give you a track record that will assure you you're in tune with your progress.

## Identify Your Support Systems, and Keep Your Dream to Yourself

Once you have your Passion Playbook, once you're touching and feeling your dream, create a support system that will help you remember that dream, and I suggest you keep your dream to yourself. Psychology studies show that if you tell people about your dream, they will acknowledge it and you will get a sense of satisfaction as if you've already achieved it. Your mind can trick your brain by such verbal acknowledgments, making you think you've already accomplished it. If this happens, you will stop before reaching your goal. If you want a support system, just do so carefully, and if you share information about your intentions, do so by saying you need to reach a certain goal and ask your support system to get on you if you don't stay with it. This also sets up a system of accountability for you.

Choose your support system carefully; remember that quitters love company. Don't choose people who are likely to be negative about your goals and encourage you to settle for the status quo. For my own support system, I select my mentors, people I look up to. You can meet with these people for a once-a-month get-together for coffee or dinner. Your support system should be a group of supporters who will listen to your dreams but also ask you about your progress toward those dreams. These are people who will be excited to share your journey with you. Once you've reached your goal, you can share it with the world, but get there first!

## Visit Your Dreams

Plan a weekly visit to your dreams so you can see and feel them; this is part of the process of locking in your plan. People may have different dreams, and some may be similar, but apply this to your desired outcome. I used to visit my NBA dream by watching games on TV and going to NBA games to watch the players live; doing that was an amazing experience. The players were so much taller and stronger than they appeared on TV. Listening to the fans cheering, the announcer speaking, and the arena rumbling after every big play was awesome. I embraced the experience and paid attention to all the details My desire became burning hot; that made a huge difference in my drive to get out there on the court myself.

The same thing happened when I visualized the homes I wanted to build. I imagined my crew and me creating and building something I had designed. Starting with a pen and a pad was one thing, but going to jobsites and seeing beautiful estates being built locked in my desire and commitment to the industry.

Dreams are intangible by nature and are hard to realize fully unless you have some sort of experience to connect with your visualization of them. Remembering my visits to NBA games and the times I watched my houses go up gives me goose bumps.

My dreams were sort of distant, and I couldn't visit them often because of my situation. Some dreams you will be able to visit a few times a month, while others, such as a marathon, might come around only once a year, but embrace these experiences whenever you can.

At first when you visit, you're going to be very excited, but after your third, fourth, or fifth visit, you're going to start feeling a little frustrated. You'll think, *I really want this. I don't want to look at it if I can't get it.* The intensity of that desire, that discomfort, will solidify your dream and make it real, and unless it's real in your mind, it won't happen.

If your dream is a new home, drive through a neighborhood you like and look at houses you'd love to own. When I was younger, I used to drive around for hours down South where I lived, look at big mansions with huge yards, and dream of living in one. It was uncomfortable in a way, but it was also a source of inspiration. I could spend time alone and dream, and that dream fed me.

I eventually built my own house, a mansion with a guarded gate and a circular driveway, a porte-cochere, and all the other things I'd dreamed of. Making your dreams manifest is an incredibly powerful thing to do. Make sure you visit your dream every single week if at all possible.

## Recitation

In addition to visiting your dreams as often as you can, recite them aloud every morning and night. Did you just think, *Is he kidding me? That's a lot of commitment every morning and night!* Yes it is. But what if you don't do it? Is it worth losing your dreams? Is it worth never achieving them?

Recitation adds the third dimension. When you recite your dreams out loud, you're no longer just seeing them in your Passion Playbook or touching them in your weekly visits, you're speaking and hearing them. Much the same way religious groups derive powerful self-affirmation from speaking their creeds, speaking your dreams gives you power.

Giving yourself positive affirmation will intensify the experience for you. Post a written list of what your plans are in your car, on your bathroom mirror, or next to your bed and recite them every morning and night.

## Exercise Drills for Creating Your Plan

 Write down the detailed timeline of your desired outcome.

 Create milestones that will keep you on track during the process.

 Specify your journey's results on a calendar.

 List people such as friends, coaches, and mentors who will help you.

 Write down the specifics about the financial obligations it will take.

 Cut out visuals of all parts of your desired outcome.

Locate, document, and attend venues where your desired outcome is at work by others who are living your dream.

 View your Passion Playbook, and recite your plan daily.

# CHAPTER

7

# TRANSFORMATION

## *Off-Season Training*

*Nothing can stop the man with the right mental attitude from achieving his goal; nothing on earth can help the man with the wrong mental attitude.*
—Thomas Jefferson

TO TRANSFORM SOMETHING MEANS DRAMATICALLY CHANGING IT IN FORM OR appearance; you have to transform yourself to live above the rim. To become successful, you have to transform yourself, to undergo a metamorphosis from who you are to who you want to become. Such a transformation will take you out of your comfort zone to where you want to go. There's no way to get where you want if you stay where you are, if you stay in your same form.

The metamorphosis a larva goes through to become a butterfly is much like what we have to go through to become successful. Our personalities start to form when we're young, and as we begin to collect experiences and be exposed to different people and environments, we become reactive.

When we start breaking out of our shells when we're teens, we're like larvae becoming caterpillars, living beings, of course, but not all we're destined to be; we're still not completely formed. Some people stay caterpillars for years if not for the rest of their lives because they fail to continue growing and transforming. The best years of such people's lives were in high school, but they're capable of so much more.

Those who want to become butterflies have to keep pushing themselves to the next level. Successful caterpillars transform themselves by building cocoons. Some people allow their negative experiences to form cocoons around them, and they stop growing and changing. Think of the many negative people around you who are constantly complaining about not being successful and not getting what they want out of life.

If you create a cocoon of positivity, of growth, you can transform what's inside and become the person you want to be. The greatness in life, achievement, and success resides in you, but it's up to you to choose the direction and the cocoon you want to grow in. Fill your environment with positive influences and people. Surround yourself with the healthy, nurturing sources of inspiration that will support your growth toward becoming a mature butterfly.

I've had to go through transformation several times in my life, once as a basketball player. I knew when I was in high school that I wanted to become a basketball player, but I had to go through a transformation to become one. Without hard work, without creating a cocoon of positive influences around me, it would have probably been impossible. The second time I had to go through a transformation was when I retired from pro sports after my son was born. I wanted to leave a legacy for my son, so I had to transform from a basketball player to a businessman who was one of the top builders and designers in the world.

To achieve such a feat, especially in such a short time, I had to go through a dramatic transformation. My metamorphosis was going to be intense; I knew this because I had already transformed myself once. It takes a lot of commitment, work, and action. I had to dig in deep; I had to surround myself with people I wanted to be like, the environment I wanted to be in, and the thoughts I wanted to think.

I had the education and talent to design and create, but becoming a builder was a different story. To get the ball rolling, I drove around for hours, studying the kinds of homes I wanted to build, and I researched the building process. I found a mentor who graciously allowed me to follow him around his projects—inside, outside, and through the entire process of building a home. I studied his every move, and I began to transform.

I submerged myself in my dream and vision. I visualized what I wanted my life to look like in five years. I made the choice to do what whatever it took to go to the top of the industry. I set my expectation that it was going to take up to five years or more of dedication to my new career to reach the success I wanted.

CHAPTER SEVEN

I acknowledged my rims at that time. A few of them included lack of building experience or portfolio in the industry, fear of failing, and the comfort of just having retired from basketball. I visualized a map, a plan of where I wanted to be from beginning to end. I set up milestones so I could test myself. I studied projects at every stage. I reviewed floor plans of existing homes to improve on them with my vision. I did this day in and day out, and I began to transform. My vision was so clear that I could complete plans in thirty days. It was time to take action. I aced the test for my contractor's license. It was really happening. I knew I could do this.

But the transformation wasn't over. I was on the site of my first project day and night. I had designed it inside and out. I was so hands-on because I was still in the process of becoming who I wanted to be. That first project wasn't perfect, but it was a strong start. After it was complete, I reviewed everything to see what had come out great and what could use improvement in the future. Such journeys are never really over.

One of my initial mistakes was thinking I had to compare my work to others' work, but then I remembered something Michael Jordan told me that changed my life: "If you want to become great at something, you can't compete against everyone else. You need to compete against yourself." This dramatic statement applies to the business world just as much as it does to the sports world. Instead of comparing my projects to the projects around them, I kept building my own visions. I kept getting better and better project after project; my homes were eventually among some of the most dramatic homes in the area where I was building. Those who came to my homes saw something totally different. They would see the experience and feel the heart and soul I had put into my projects. If I had continued to use others' work as my benchmarks, I could easily have stopped short of what I could have otherwise achieved. Instead, people often told me they'd never seen anything like my homes.

Once again, I had become something totally different, but without my intense belief in and commitment to the necessity of change, it wouldn't have happened. I had to be open to the sometimes painful and always arduous process of transformation, the metamorphosis from one identity to the next.

TRANSFORMATION

## Transformation Is a Journey, Not a Moment

People often talk about what they want to do, what they're going to do, and then they say the magic word that keeps them in their place—*but*. That's a word that stops you from changing the direction of your life. You can't transform with *but*; that's an excuse. "I want to become successful, but I have this job." "I want to be successful, but I just don't have enough money today."

*When* is another word that can stop you. "I'm going to become successful when I get more money." "I'm going to become successful when I'm ready." Success doesn't wait for anyone; it's up to you to choose success. Once you've done so, once you've exposed the thief, you can transform yourself.

True transformation occurs in the journey; the metamorphosis happens along the way. You don't expect to sit at the CEO's desk on your first day in business and have any real shot at performing effectively and successfully. You have to put in the time, learn about the business, and work your way up. As you gain experience, you become smarter, more efficient, more managerial. You end up with the skills and experience you need to run a company. Without undergoing a transformation, you cannot be who you want to be or get what you want out of life.

I'll mention different types of transformation you'll need on your journey to a new you.

## Personal Transformation

Your personal transformation, the first transformation you'll undergo on your journey to your goal, comes from competing with yourself. Evaluate your past achievements and set out to better them each time you're on the court. First, you must expose the thief as mentioned in chapter 5. This allows you to establish a new baseline and get out of your own way. People who aren't aware of this part of the process end up all over the board and frustrated big time because they feel as though they're doing everything but not getting the results they wanted. Take bite-sized chunks when dealing with this process so you don't get overwhelmed. Concentrate on small achievements every day, elements of the process you can control.

People have a misconception that when their surroundings change, they will change and their situation will improve. It's the opposite. When you change from inside, you will project this, and your surroundings will change as a result. What you read, listen to, and do are all part of personal transformation.

## Get Your Attitude in Check

A positive attitude is a priceless help in personal transformation in that it affects how you perceive tasks. If your success plan includes becoming fit because of its positive benefits, you might have to get up an hour earlier than usual to exercise. As we all know, the beginning of a workout plan is always tough; it takes a while to get in the groove. If you focus on how much you don't want to get up that early, you'll find it tough to start and stick with your fitness plan. But if you focus on the fact that this action is one step that you can control and will positively affect your outcome, you will adjust to the program quicker and be more productive.

A bad attitude can hinder performance and derail success. A bad attitude usually comes from negative past experiences, low self-esteem, stress, fear, anger, and even resistance to change. Not only can a bad attitude take you down, it can also take down the people around you. Those with bad attitudes are almost always negative, always viewing the glass as half empty, always speaking negatively about situations and even those around them. Each time they express their negativity, they're projecting that negativity into their own futures. The power of our words is enormous; they can create a straight line between us and success, or they can call down destruction on us and our futures.

## Replace Wasted Time with Personal Growth

Choosing to avoid that which does not help us toward our desired outcomes is a great and efficient start toward personal growth. Consider all the time you spend driving. According to the Federal Highway Administration, we spend thirty-four hours per year in traffic, not to mention much more if you include total drive time going to and from your daily destination. The time we spend behind the wheel can be put to good use. Instead of listening to music, we could be listening to personal growth CDs.

## *Exercise Regularly*

Get on an exercise regimen; exercise has obvious physical benefits, but you might not realize how important it is for success. Numerous studies report that exercise increases retention and learning. You will think clearer, feel better, sleep better, and have more energy, which you will need when you start ramping up your schedule to reach your goal and stay there.

## Transform Your Environment

Second, just as a caterpillar has to, you have to create a different environment that will allow you to transform, and your existing environment will not allow you to do that. This doesn't mean you have to disconnect yourself completely from your current environment or the people in it; it means you have to start replacing your current environment with the environment you want to be in because you will rise to the level of the environment you're in. Surround yourself with people who are striving for success, including those you know but don't spend time with, and new people. Join networks geared toward your success goal to exchange ideas and meet motivated people. Take a look at your environment to see where and how you can make it more organized. Successful people have systems. Systems that work require order; if your surroundings are a mess, that could be a reflection on how your life is going.

## Transform Your Organization

Finally, you have to transform how you communicate with react to, and influence people. Your organizations include your job, church, clubs, or groups in which you have to interact with people to reach common goals. Building and maintaining healthy, effective relationships with those you work with is a key to organizational success. How you communicate and interact with your peers can determine the level of success you will have with the missions you share in your groups. You're seeking a balance with these interactions; extremes can work against you, so be careful not to communicate to much or too little. Some reserved people don't like communicating; this may be okay when it's just you, but in a group, such an attitude can hold you back. Try opening up, communicating, and finding common ground with your peers to establish baseline communications.

Generally, when you communicate with your coworkers or colleagues in a group, it's to complete a task, so shake it up a bit and every once and a while ask others how their days are going. Ask how you can help make their jobs easier or more efficient. Get to know them better by taking them to lunch once in a while. Remember their birthdays and anniversaries and details about their families. When colleagues do something good, express excitement for them, and show gratitude if they assist you with something even if it is their job. By acknowledging their accomplishments and helping them through their mistakes, you will show leadership qualities and exhibit goodwill.

If you are a leader of your group, you can help them transform themselves by sharing a vision of an environment that will benefit everyone. It starts with you, so lead by example. People will watch what you do more than they will listen to what you say. Post positive quotes and messages in your group environment by well-known, successful people and a few by people you may respect and look up to but might not be well known. The physiological effect of this will affect others' attitudes and morale. A positive environment is infectious, and it promotes unity. The seeds you plant will sprout throughout your organization and bear fruit that benefits everyone.

When you combine these types of transformations, you will be in a position to evolve, get the most out of yourself, and create success throughout your life.

## Transformation Drills

 **_Watch Out for Your Thief._** Expose what items your thief is responsible for that are holding you back, and write what actions you will take to combat them so you will control your thief.

***Absorb Your Vision.*** Write down your desired outcome below and recite it daily.

 ***Grow Personally.*** Write down the time of day you will read personal-growth books and listen to audio CDs.

 ***Create a Transformation Environment.*** Update your environment by posting positive quotes in your office and home. Replace items from the past with vision or dream items. Write down what your perfect would be.

 ***Elevate Your Success Relationships.*** Improve your social environment by actively seeking out success-minded people.

 ***Keep Your Stats.*** Keep a daily workout log that includes your short- and long-term goals.

# CHAPTER

# ACCOUNTABILITY

## *Review Your Stats*

*Discipline is the bridge between goals and accomplishment.*
—Jim Rohn

SAY WHAT YOU MEAN, AND DO WHAT YOU SAY YOU WILL. DO THE RIGHT things, and the right things will happen. You've heard this before. Some people call it a kind of Golden Rule, but there's a surprising lack of accountability and integrity in the world today in business and personal matters and everywhere in between.

Accountability is a key ingredient to success in living your life above the rim; it can make the difference between just dreaming your dream and living it. Accountability means taking responsibility for your dream by mixing your words and vision with controlled, scheduled action to achieve your objective.

## Non-Accountability Has Liabilities

Not being accountable can be a real liability in many situations, especially in business. This is very prevalent in the construction industry. Imagine having new blueprints and a vision to build a gorgeous dream home. You've spent years dreaming and developing it, and now you're going to start construction. But a problem crops up—you discover that budget quotes and completion dates are just verbal estimates, and the contractor has no accountability to you or the construction manager. Your project starts veering off track. Your date for breaking ground gets pushed back a few days, and then a few more days, and then two weeks due to a lack of accountability.

Once construction gets underway, you encounter issues on the jobsite. The manager has left the jobsite and expects the contractor to do the work properly, but the contractor is running into issues on the jobsite that require the manager's presence if delays are to be avoided. Without the manager's presence, problems and delays keep piling up.

This kind of lack of accountability could turn any project into a train wreck. You started off two weeks late, and every subcontractor, from groundbreaking and foundation to framing, preplumb, prewire, and drywall get frustrated with delay upon delay.

Eventually, you could be six months to a year off schedule, which adds up to more than frustration–it could cost you a lot more money. Your bank will not care about the excuses your construction crew feeds you; it will just charge you the interest that keeps piling up. If you're taking six months to a year extra, you're talking about being over budget dramatically. If your manager is not the accountable type, the whole project can become one big blaming game.

## Accountability Has Benefits

Contrast a lack of accountability with accountability. An organized manager presents you with a schedule. The budget has been bid up properly, and agreements and contracts have proper signatures. Contactors, subcontractors—everyone, including yourself—knows all the details. The entire project has been visualized and has been virtually prebuilt before it even breaks ground. You feel comfortable when the general contractor says, "If something goes wrong, I'll take care of it. I'll make sure it's fixed."

How much better would your project go if you started on time? And because of your accountability system and the fact that the general contractor is actually overseeing the project and being accountable, you probably will come out under budget or at budget with a better result than you expected.

This is just a simple example of how accountability works in the construction industry, but the most important place for accountability is in your life. The more time you waste being unaccountable to yourself, your environment, your family, and your relationships, the more time you will lose. The goal is to be as efficient as possible so you can achieve the most you can out of your life and live a fulfilled, successful life.

## Hold Yourself Accountable to Yourself

*Webster's* defines accountability as an obligation or willingness to accept responsibility or to account for one's actions. Odds are you probably already had a good understanding of what it means to be accountable even without *Webster's* help, but do you actually live a life of accountability? I'm not perfect, and we're all guilty of not being accountable all the time. But if we have a goal of increasing our levels of accountability, we'll end up completely accountable to whatever it is we set out to do. This will allow us to live above the rim and achieve whatever success we want.

Understanding the cost of not being accountable is one of the best ways to start a conversation on accountability because we're used to talking about it but not used to discussing the consequences of its lack. No one wants to discuss his or her failures, just his or her successes. But understanding that failure sometimes can be your best friend is one of the best ways to become successful. The more you fail, the more you will succeed.

Lack of personal accountability leads to personal dysfunction. If you're not accountable to yourself, you will easily get off track when it comes to pursuing your goals or even fail to achieve them despite your best intentions. Your goal gets thrown into the graveyard of dreams.

What's the impact on you personally? If you keep setting goals but lack accountability, you'll quickly develop a lack of confidence in your ability to actually achieve your goals. These will dramatically impact your self-esteem; the thief within will start saying you're a failure. But in reality, you were just not accountable to your goal.

Let's say you have a goal of losing twenty pounds in three months. You're on track, working hard, and doing well. But one night, you're out with friends, having a good time, and your friends say, "Just have one! It won't hurt. You're looking so good. You've done so well. You need to reward yourself." If you haven't yet lost that twenty pounds, rewarding yourself too early can throw you off track. And you know that rewarding yourself for successfully *losing* weight by eating food that causes you to *gain* weight is simply moronic.

But you say, "I'll just have one. It won't make a difference." An hour later, it tasted so good that you have another. The immediate results won't be obvious, but over the next couple of days, because you didn't see any immediate disruption, you decide to have another. Before you know it, you've ended up cheating four or five times in ten days. If you continue this process, not only will you not make your goal of losing twenty pounds, you may actually gain weight. Not reaching your goal on your date will result in a lack of confidence, and you'll feel you've failed. The thief becomes more powerful.

When you hear the voice in your head saying, *It's okay. Just have one*, you should immediately determine why you heard that and go into action: Check your accountability system. Look at your track record. Review your plan for success. Use every accountability resource at your disposal to stay on track and keep the thief locked down.

I know you can identify with this struggle—it's universal. We've all fallen short at one time or another and have failed to hold ourselves accountable. This became all too real in my own life while running my companies and chasing success. The ironic part about this is that we often consider success as making tons of money, but what good is all that money if you're not around to enjoy it? Because of my accountability to my businesses, I was making millions, but because I lacked accountability to myself, my health was deteriorating. I just had to become accountable to myself.

## Integrity and Accountability

One reason people struggle with accountability is due to a lack of integrity. *Webster's* defines integrity as a quality of being honest and having strong moral principles, moral uprightness, and being whole and undivided. Accountability cannot be achieved without personal integrity. Think of your initial goal as 100 percent. If you aren't accountable due to lack of integrity, that 100 percent turns into 98 percent and then 92 percent. Each time you cheat or go off track from you goal, your integrity weakens more.

Think about integrity as a bicycle wheel, a tire supported by a whole lot of spindly spokes. Such a wheel with all its spokes will give you a comfortable, easy ride, but each time you lose a bit of integrity, one of the spokes is removed. Each time you make a mistake and don't own up to it, you sacrifice a spoke of integrity. You probably won't notice a difference in the way your bike rides with just one or two missing spokes, but over time, as more spokes go, the wheel will not have enough support to hold its shape. You'll start experiencing a sluggish, bumpy ride, and finally, your wheel will collapse. To reach your goals, you have to start from within so you don't lose the spokes of integrity. You need 100 percent of your wheel.

You can see the results of the lack of integrity all around—in business, politics, religion, and our communities. When people operate without integrity, the long-term effects are dramatic. Having true integrity is one of the first steps to becoming personally accountable.

## Accountability to Family

In life above the rim, your success is not only financial; it also involves your family. In family, different types of accountability make a difference in success. Accountable communication in a family can create happiness and success in it.

We are all responsible for how we communicate with each other, especially our family members. In a perfect world, all families would be loving, supportive, and full of positive feedback for one another. In such a family, when you fall short of a goal or slide off track in your journey, you will get feedback such as, "I'm so glad you took on the task of changing your life and achieving your goal. Even though we all fall off track sometimes, you're still way ahead of where you'd have been if you hadn't started." Such nurturing feedback will inspire you to get back on track and keep on working.

But every family is different, and while some families seem to have nothing but support and positivity for one another, many families are programmed to offer only negative feedback. When you know if you get off track that your family will say, "I told you that you couldn't do it" or "Looks like your falling off track as always," it's understandable that you will feel reluctant to be accountable to them. But even their negative feedback can be turned into a positive by using it as fuel to help you succeed.

Negative statements are frequently demeaning and hurtful, but if you look at every experience as an opportunity to gain something positive, this will dramatically increase the value of your experiences. You can respond to your family's negative comments, "You're right. I obviously needed to be more accountable since I'm getting off track." You could turn the fear of hearing their negative comments into the desire to be more accountable to your system. It's sometimes better to avoid certain people altogether if their feedback becomes so harmful and demotivating that you become angry, depressed, or argumentative, but now that you've exposed your thief, it will get easier to remove the fear of negativity from your family relationships.

Our accountability for our communication becomes even more important in our immediate family; we have to teach our children how to communicate properly because this will be a quality that will help them the rest of their lives. If you're not aware of this, you can set your children up for failure in communicating without even trying. Children absorb more of what we do more than of what we say. If you tell them not to curse, drink, smoke, or yell but you're doing all those things, they will learn those behaviors from you without your having to breathe a word. This can move from generation to generation if no one embraces the concept and takes action against it. Kids who can't express themselves properly can become frustrated or reserved and can suffer from lack of confidence or the inability to bond emotionally or resolve conflicts. It could also result in poor language skills or even mental problems that can lead to depression and social anxiety. We want better for our kids, and they deserve better, so we need to be accountable for teaching them to communicate properly.

## Accountability to Friends

Friends can also make demands on your drive to be accountable. While you stay family even when family members are negative toward you, you don't have to keep negative friends. You can choose to surround yourself with only those friends who want you to succeed. Don't make yourself accountable to friends who like you just where you are and would be uncomfortable if you started achieving greater things. Look for friends who, like you, are always trying to achieve more; those are the friends to keep close. Take a step back from acquaintances who seem disgruntled, unfulfilled, or stagnant.

You generally see your friends during your leisure time. Because friend time equates to fun time, your accountability is reinforced by the fact that you want to enjoy the time you spend with friends; you don't want to show up feeling uncomfortable about not living up to the goals you set for yourself. That motivation coupled with the support and encouragement that friends can offer will help keep you in line with the system you've set up for yourself.

## Accountability to Your Community

Learning to be accountable to the public or your community can be of great personal benefit. Your community can be local or worldwide; it can consist of groups, clubs, or online communities built on social media platforms. You can offer assistance, support, and mentorship to those who fall in line with the dreams you're achieving. As you draw support, encouragement, and feedback from such a large pool, you'll also receive a massive amount of positive reinforcement that will boost you on your journey as well as others you're assisting. You'll be surprised how much you'll change yourself and develop a desire to be accountable as you assist others.

Community accountability is especially popular among people who are trying to get into shape. They'll start a blog or some sort of community source online so they can track their progress. They'll get a lot of positive feedback, much more than they could have gotten from any one or two people. A strong community is a powerful source of accountability.

## Accountability to Your Mentor

The most important type of accountability is to a coach or a mentor. Generally, a coach or a mentor has a vested interest in your success. Setting up weekly meetings with coaches or mentors will allow you to actively track your progress. This will give you structured, results-oriented, positive feedback that can help you stay on a system of accountability and help you reach your goals much more efficiently.

Coaches and mentors will also tell you exactly how it is. Instead of telling you things they think you *want* to hear, which sometimes family and friends will do, they'll tell you what you *need* to hear about your progress. Real talk from a respected source will keep you in touch with reality and keep your perception unskewed.

I've had many accountability partners, but some of the best were the coaches I've played for. I've had accountability partners in the business world; one in particular was among the best I've ever had. While I was developing my career in real estate development, I learned that being on the jobsite every day was not a healthy lifestyle. For the first year or so, I was okay because I had played pro sports for ten years and my body was revved up so high I'd burn off anything I ate. But over time, eating garbage on jobsites, settling for fast food, and eating late at night started taking a toll. I started getting out of shape and gaining an unhealthy amount of weight—I was making millions but losing my health. I took responsibility for myself. I realized that even though I'd been a pro athlete, I'd obviously gotten way off track or I wouldn't be so out of shape. So I hired an accountability coach, one of the best in the industry. He was feared by most professional athletes because he was firm, strict, tough, and always on task; he looked for and demanded massive results with his clients.

His name is Mack Newton, one of the most amazing individuals you could ever meet. He was very honest with me; he put me on a system that allowed me to achieve while taking into account where I was starting from.

Having an accountability coach tell me the truth rebooted reality for me. I woke up to where I actually was. He pointed out that if I didn't change my life and direction, I would become increasingly unhealthy and might not be around much longer. That sobered me quickly; I had a young son and a wife I loved dearly.

An important fact about Mack is that he was not cheap; that forced me to stick to the system so I would ensure results and not waste money and time. As well, I really wanted to be on his wall of fame!

As we got underway, the program challenged me, but I started thriving right away because of my desire for the structure and accountability I'd had during my basketball days. I realized that I had missed being challenged. Within three months, I lost fifty-four pounds and increased my numbers to that of a healthier person. The more I progressed and stayed true to his system, the more I was rewarded. The weekly weigh-ins I had and the meal sheets I turned into him let me know I was going in the right direction. My reward was in the mirror, and that reward went right to my soul. I became sharper and more focused as well.

Now, fifty-four pounds in three months probably sounds like too much too fast, but keep in mind that I'm six nine, so my weight goals are different from what someone five ten would have.

You can see how positive a coaching influence has been in my life. I'm healthier, I can think a lot more clearly, and I am able to perform at a higher level. I'm not exhausted as I once was. I'm more energetic for my family. My regimen worked out for so many positive reasons. But without an accountability partner, a coach, a mentor, it would have been difficult.

Not just anyone can be your mentor. If you wanted to become a doctor, you wouldn't take on an accountant as a mentor. If you wanted to be a racecar driver, you wouldn't ask a swim coach to mentor you. Whatever your goal is, choose mentors who align with it.

Be careful when it comes to choosing mentors; there are too many would-be mentors who don't live by their mentoring. We've all seen this plenty of times, and I've also been guilty of not following my own advice at earlier times in my career. If you're looking for a health and fitness mentor, an overweight coach probably wouldn't be the best choice. I chose a fitness mentor full of integrity and discipline who looked the part and had a history of success. The wrong mentor will probably not get you on track and could indeed get you off track.

Set up meetings with your mentor to go over your progress and keep yourself accountable; this will give your mentor the chance to measure your progress and make changes in your action plan as necessary. This doesn't just apply to fitness goals but to all your goals.

ACCOUNTABILITY

Your mentor will tell you that you need a system. Most people go to their mentors without a system; those with solid, workable systems in place would probably not need mentors. If your mentor doesn't provide you with a system, you can develop one using the success principles in this book. In the "action guide" in my *Life above and beyond the Rim* success transformation system, I lay out exactly how to develop a system that will help you achieve your goals, how to choose mentors, and everything else you'll need to become successful.

Let's understand the importance of systems. You're exposed to systems on a daily basis. You wake up, have your coffee, get your kids ready, and prepare to go to work. You have many more systems there established by your boss. You have a system of paperwork for your supervisor. You're used to dealing with systems, but the most important system is your system of life. You have to be accountable to your life and to the personal goals you want to reach. When you fail, it's often because you didn't have a system.

## Accountability Drills

Let's address systems that you can be accountable to. I gave you a few examples earlier, but let's start with creating a daily checklist using my *Life above the Rim* system. The ten principles in this book form a great guideline for you to create a checklist for daily use.

Three keys to know that you're creating the proper checklist are visual, verbal, and tangible; you want to see, hear, and feel them. Using all these senses will allow for a great impact that will register psychologically.

### *Visual*

You want to be able to see your checklist because seeing is believing. To generate a visual representation of your system, write it down, and I recommend you do so every day. Think of it as a high-level to-do list. Many days, you'll be writing the same thing over and over, but that will etch it into your mind.

## Verbal

Recite what you're holding yourself accountable to daily. Again, you're saturating your brain with your message.

## Tangible

Make your accountability real and results-based, something you can touch or feel emotionally and physically. You can integrate tangibility into your accountability with something as simple as a checklist that allows you to mark off successes and track your performance.

Creating tangible accountability will affect you and the people you care about. Even small things that allow you to establish a positive goal achievement can move you toward greater things. If you ask your spouse, "How can I make your day easier?" she (in my case) might say, "You could wash the dishes every once in a while, or make the bed on occasion, or do the laundry." Set up a system that allows you to check off the things you've committed to doing each day to make your partner's day a little better. You'll derive from that a tangible accomplishment that builds toward your attitude for success, and you'll have made your partner happier.

## Overwriting

If your life could be compared to an old VHS tape or the hard drive on your computer, overwriting means wiping out the bad experiences of the past by recording new material over them. Instead of using fear-based accountability by attaching your new goals to old, negative experiences, use the initial, small accomplishments you achieve with your new accountability system to replace past negative experiences or failures with positive successes you can build on for the future. Use the visual, verbal, and tangible tools at your disposal to completely wipe out the old and overwrite it with the new.

## Accountability Checklist Drills

 Find an accountability partner or mentor.

 Create daily, weekly, and monthly accountability checklists.

 Track your progress using times, dates, and accomplishments.

 Write down your desired outcome and read them daily.

# CHAPTER

# 9

# TAKE ACTION

## *Take the Shot*

*Action is the foundational key to all success.*
—Pablo Picasso

*Some people want it to happen, some wish it would happen, and others make it happen.*
—Michael Jordan

**D**ON'T BE A SPECTATOR—GET OUT OF THE STANDS AND INTO THE GAME OF your life by taking action. You can visualize and plan gigantic dreams, but without action, they're nothing. You can make the critical choice to be successful, but without action, your choices are meaningless. You can set expectations, but without action, they're nothing. You can identify your rims, you can expose the thief, you can begin transformation, you can be accountable, but action is the catalyst; it's what makes dreams reality.

## Get in the Game

Many people don't take action; they get what's called analysis paralysis. They research the dream, plan it, and do all the things they can around what they want to do—but they fail to act.

The word *action* has many definitions, but its root is *act*—changing, doing something. It's the all-important transition from nonmovement to movement. Action will change your life by moving it from a state of wanting, believing, and hoping to a state of doing. You'll never realize your dreams by standing still. If your desired outcome is important, your actions will show it.

*Action Expresses Priorities.*
—Mahatma Gandhi

## Action vs. Conversation

In a small town in Michigan, four good friends, "musketeers" they called themselves, worked for the same paper company. They'd been best friends since grade school and did everything together. They worked very hard. Even though they lived at opposite ends of town and worked in different departments of their huge company, every Friday, they met at Murphy's, a bar and eatery in their hometown that offered one-dollar beers during happy hour.

More important, they loved meeting with each other; it gave them an opportunity to really talk and discuss everything from politics to sports, but it seemed they would always end up talking about what they were going to do someday to change their lives for the better.

"One day I'm going to save up enough to start my own business. I'll make my own rules and make sure my employees get more vacation days so they can spend more time with their families," John said.

The other guys nodded their approval. "Boy, that sure would be nice," one responded. Each guy shared his vision of his future, what he planned to do one day, and how it was going to be so awesome.

These Friday get-togethers went on for weeks, months. Over time, one of the group started getting quiet, uncomfortable, and even sort of antsy during their discussions. John asked, "Hey Steve, you okay? You seem a little distant lately."

"No, I'm okay. I'm just taking it all in," Steve replied.

They continued week after week until one Friday, Steve didn't show up. The others didn't think much of it and launched into their usual conversation.

The next week, Steve wasn't there again. The guys started getting concerned. As the weeks went by, they even started getting a little resentful.

Five years went by, and the three musketeers were still meeting at Murphy's on Fridays and talking about what they were going to do someday. All of a sudden, in walked Steve. The guys were surprised. John was the first to speak. "Look who just walked in! Where have you been? I was looking for your face on a milk carton!" The other two expressed exactly the same sentiments.

"Well," Steve began, "you know how we always met and talked about what we were going to do one day? Well, I made the choice to do it! I took some of my savings and started a consulting business. Over the last five years, my business has grown, and I've traveled all over the United States. I'm back in town to move my family to Florida to our new house, and I wanted to say good-bye and thank you for all the Fridays we used to dream together."

The others looked on in disbelief, excited and sad at the same time. It seemed they instantly realized their lives were going to stay the same or even get worse if they didn't make choices, take action, as Steve had done.

When you start taking action, your life might not change 100 percent overnight; you most likely won't achieve your goal in an instant. But the direction of your life will change instantly, and will be actively directed toward your goal.

Dreaming dreams and making the choice to go for goals is a kind of action, but dreams and mental decisions don't create reality. Until your feet move, until the rubber hits the road, you're not progressing toward your destiny.

Andrew Carnegie said, "As I grow older, I pay less attention to what people say and I watch what they do." That's a good one. How many times have you seen people say they're going to do this or that? You can truly know what they are only by watching their actions.

How many possible doctors, musicians, and astronauts never existed because the people who had such dreams failed to take action? How many unrealized dreams are floating around in people's heads unrealized for lack of action?

> *"As I grow older, I pay less attention to what*
> *people say. I just watch what they do."*
> —Andrew Carnegie

## Procrastination: The Opposite of Action

As Brian Tracy stated in his book *Eat that Frog*, you have to eat the frog. I love the book. That "frog" is whatever you need to do to make progress. Mr. Tracy's idea is that the first thing you should do every morning is whatever will move you forward. Eat that frog. I love the spirit of action and forward motion he imparts. Instead of putting off the tough things until you've finished up the little stuff, tackle them first, not at the end of the day when you're tired, out of time, and unable to do them well—if at all.

Procrastination engenders personal paralysis. You'll hear people say, "I'll get to it later" or my favorite, "I'll do that when …" I've fallen victim to procrastination myself; I didn't escape that victim status until I started to do something.

Obvious, right? But writing down your goals is only part of the process, as is visualizing it; actually doing it is what will make it happen. When you understand that, put all these principles together, and use them in harmonious sequence, amazing things will happen.

Procrastinating when you should be acting will damage your confidence. Inertia creates insecurity, which can be deadly if you're insecure and lack confidence you can do something. Over time, you will *not* do it, and worse, you'll end up believing you *can't* do it.

Procrastinating will allow you to create the negative habit of making excuses, which will only defer success. Excuses are like cutting off limbs on your tree of success. When you make an excuse, you defer your accomplishment. Success is organic, just like life. So many people are reaching for success; it's absolutely devastating for you to defer. You're cutting off a branch of growth from your tree of success.

One of my personal characteristics I fought with and still fight with at times is trying to be too organized, too ready, too prepared before I take action. This could be a good thing because such preparation could decrease the chances of making mistakes as you act and becoming discouraged in the process. But at some point, overanalyzing the situation will cause you to lose ground and waste time. What you put off today won't have the chance to start ripening today.

What's the worst that could happen if you just took action? You might find out that you could have or should have taken a bit more or a bit less action. But if you started at zero, took action, and achieved 20 percent of what you were shooting for, it doesn't matter that you had planned to be 30 percent done by that time. The fact that you took action means you're 20 percent there.

Visualizing and writing down goals is part of the loop that is completed only when you take action. That will embed your dream deep in your heart. You stop being about the goal; the goal starts being about you.

Procrastination comes with a particularly high price tag for leaders because people follow strength, not weakness. If you're an indecisive leader who can't take action, people will not follow you. Some leaders have had imperfect plans, but because they took action, they were able to accomplish great things and became well known.

On the other side of that coin are people with amazing ideas and brilliant plans who fail to act; no one will ever know their visions.

## What's Stopping You?

One of the primary reasons people don't act is fear they can't do it, fear of a past experience, or fear of failing. If you find yourself procrastinating, fear is around somewhere close. But fear is made up; it's internal. Fear is as large as you let it get. If you start from the beginning, work through the system, and apply the principles in *Life above the Rim*, the chances of fear standing in your way will be pretty slim.

Understand that fear cannot stand up to persistence; action and positive thinking will eventually overcome fear. The best way to get rid of fear is to act. Act on your fear, eat the frog, take steps for advancement, and face your fear head on. Retreat is not an option; it engenders only more fear and erodes your integrity, confidence, and self-esteem.

## What Are Your Fears?

Fear generated by past experiences is a common obstacle to action. You may have had negative experiences during your previous attempts to take action. But if you acted and failed, you can learn something from that process. Those experiences make you a better person and better at the process going forward. Acting against fear is far superior to succumbing to analysis paralysis. This was summed up perfectly by Hall of Famer Wayne Gretzky: "You miss 100 percent of shots you don't take."

Others' negativity also creates fear, and this can cause that paralysis. Again, you can combat negativity by taking action. Negative people will affect your outcome if you take ownership of their comments and give up on action.

Another source of fear is a lack of plan or direction. If you don't know where you're going, you won't know when you get there. Imagine going through a maze and having no idea where you're going. After three, four, five, six turns, your anxiety is building. You're lost in the middle of nowhere and don't know how to get out. That's the way a lot of people feel when they start a mission or a goal without a plan or direction.

But imagine going through that same maze knowing what turns to take and how long it should take. When you're taking those turns, the anxiety is not there. You're not afraid because you know you're going to get out and even when you're going to get out because you've planned.

When I decided to make it to the NBA, I wrote down a plan and went over it until it was engraved on my mind. It became so powerful that it fostered my belief in myself—my outcome had been planned. Whenever I would feel fear setting in, I took action. I would run in the middle of the night; I knew I was doing more than the average, thereby increasing my chances of success. When I faced adversity, fear wasn't a problem because I knew my outcome; I knew where I was going.

Lack of self-belief caused by memories of experiences, present circumstances, or a dystopic view of the future will affect your ability to do, but action cures this type of fear as well. When you start putting one foot in front of the other, you start creating a new sense of being; you start rewriting the script of what your mind has told you. Each positive step you take, each milestone you achieve through action will strengthen your belief.

I've experienced all these fears in my life, but I've also put into practice the principles that allowed me to overcome anything in my way. In the process of writing this book, I revisited all the principles in my life. The fear of others not valuing my message was something I had to overcome. Even though I've used these principles to reach success and have coached business professionals to do the same, I've still had to battle that thief within telling me no one would listen. In reality, people all around the world have benefitted from other people's stories of their mistakes and their successes alike!

When I met those agents in Chicago who made decisions that didn't support my career goals, I had to terminate that relationship, and that was a big step. Many people would have been afraid to make that choice because they would have felt they didn't have leverage and were alone; they would fear losing out altogether if they didn't accept the offer.

But I had to make a decision. I believed in where I was going. I sat in an apartment with the defecting assistant. I was really destroyed, depressed, and upset, but I still had that burning desire to succeed. I knew if I didn't take action, things would get only worse. I got in the mix of the action. Because of that, the window opened and opportunity presented itself.

I had to take action to create my companies after I retired from pro sports. Just the desire to make lots of money in real estate wouldn't cut it; I needed to take action. When I retired, no one was waiting for me with a great job; I had to pursue opportunities to create one for myself. Through action, through constant pursuit of my goal, I completed my first project, then another, and then another. I was quickly on my way to success as a builder.

Whatever you do just take steps forward. Take action every day, every week, and every year. Don't let your dreams sit on the sidelines and eventually die in the dream graveyard because it's already too full.

## Take-Action Drills

Martin Luther King Jr. said, "If you can't fly, then run. If you can't run, then walk. If you can't walk, then crawl. But whatever you do, you have to keep moving forward."

Think about what action looks like for you. Think about your dreams, your goals, and your desires. What steps do you need to take to make them happen? When you understand that you can design your life and that action makes it happen, when you create the blueprint and when you recite, believe, visualize, and take action on your blueprint, you can design the life you want.

- Review the previous principles. You need to understand the principles leading up to this point so your actions will be effective.

- Review your action plan. It should clearly lay out a beginning, middle, and an end of your goal.

- Base your actions on results that you list in a daily system, a daily plan to move you toward your goal. Don't be fooled by positive things that don't move you toward your goal. If your sales goal is to sell a certain amount per week, figure out how many calls you'll have to make every day and make them; don't let yourself get tied up in calls that last for hours. If they don't produce results, they're just long phone calls that keep you from calling other leads.

One of the things I needed to do when I first began training for pro ball was to increase my shooting percentage. I did very well. I was very athletic. I was able to jump and dunk the ball and make exciting plays, but to get into and then stay in the NBA, I had to balance the equation by being a shooter.

Not realizing it at the time, I went to the principles in this book. I needed a results-based plan to ensure my success. I started by dreaming of being one of the best shooters in the NBA and by visualizing how I would achieve that status. I saw myself making shots one by one, shooting with ease and comfort. I made the choice to have the best shooting percentage on the team no matter what that took. I set realistic expectations; I knew it was going to take a lot of work and sacrifice. While other players were enjoying themselves, I'd have to be in the gym.

I acknowledged my glass ceiling, my rim, by looking at my current shooting percentage and calculating how many shots a day I'd have to take and more important—make. I studied my films and discovered the reasons I made shots and missed them. I studied top shooters in the league and began to transform myself. I created a shot log of makes to misses to become accountable for the time I was in the gym. I wanted to ensure my time wasn't wasted.

Finally, it was time to take action—actually put up shots. The only way I was going to get better was to go through the motion repeatedly. When I started focusing on the shots I made, I started paying more attention and working hard on making more of those shots, which in turn increased my percentage of shots made. By the next season, I had increased my shooting percentage dramatically.

When I was designing and building homes, I needed to make sure they weren't great only in my own mind, so how long it took to build them and to sell them and how much profit each sale yielded were the data I collected. That data told me I was doing the right things. I worked hard at this equation until I could build and produce the most efficient project. I got to a point that my houses delivered more value per square foot than almost any others in the area.

Whatever your goal is, taking results-based action will put the power in your hands and increase your percentage of success.

> *The proper function of man is to live, not to exist. I shall not*
> *waste my days in trying to prolong them. I shall use my time.*
> —Jack London

## Taking-Action Drills

 *Positive Actions*

- Declare responsibility of your outcome and recite your goal daily.

- Take daily action toward your desired outcome.

- Create and maintain a to-do list.

- Be accountable; track your results both good and bad.

- Spend fifteen to thirty minutes a day studying the habits of those who have achieved your goal.

- Visualize yourself achieving your desired outcome.

- Try to improve on your results every week and track them.

- Work out at least thirty minutes four to five times a week.

 *Negative Actions*

- procrastinating and putting off working on your goal

- winging it and not tracking your progress

- telling everyone what you plan to do instead of taking action

- blaming others for you not taking action

- quitting

- getting opinions to justify negative feelings

 *Time-Wasting Actions*

- overanalyzing too much instead of acting

- sleeping in too late (instead, get up earlier, and exercise to start off your day)

- e-mailing all day

- tending to minimal disruptions and putting off positive actions

- spending too much time on social media

- wasting time on things you can't control

- repeating your mistakes

- dwelling on the past

- feeling entitled

- watching more than two hours of TV a day

# CHAPTER

# 10

# EMPOWERING
# OTHERS

## *Pass to the Open Man*

*If your actions inspire others to dream more, learn more,
do more and become more, you are a leader.*
—John Quincy Adams

A LL GREAT LEADERS KNOW THE ART OF EMPOWERMENT BECAUSE OTHERS empowered and gave them the chance that propelled them to success.

It was 1993; I had just come off the road with the Phoenix Suns' Summer League team I had joined while they were on the road. Assistant coach Lionel Hollins, who opened the door for me to play on the Summer League team, went to Jerry Colangelo, the Suns' owner/general manager and spoke highly of me, saying they should try to make room to sign me. My next stop was going to be the Los Angeles Clippers. Though I would have been happy to play for the Clippers, the Suns were the second-best team in the league at that time; they had lost the championship to the Chicago Bulls the year before, when I was with the Bulls. It would be amazing to play back-to-back for the two best teams in the world. I got a meeting with Mr. Colangelo to plead my case and get a deal. I flew to Phoenix for the meeting with a particular feeling in my stomach and soul. My life's purpose was somehow here.

The time came for my meeting with one of the best-known figures in pro sports. He leaned back and asked me, "I heard you played well, but why should I take a chance on you with our team when we have a full roster"? At that point, I had nothing to lose. I had put it all on the line to get there; no turning back. I said, "Gather your best players and watch me play. If you don't think I'm worth your time, I'll be on the first plane to LA and sign with the Clippers." He leaned forward and said, "Kid, I like the fire in your eyes."

He called a special workout, and several of the team's best players were there in minutes, ready to go. The game started. Mr. Colangelo was in the stands watching this confident kid looking to make a name for himself.

I gave it all I had, putting on display dunks, jump shots, spin moves— every tool I had. After over thirty minutes of play, Mr. Colangelo stopped the play and said he'd seen enough. "You're not going to LA, son, because you're now going to be wearing a Phoenix Suns Jersey!"

I'm forever thankful to Jerry Colangelo for empowering me and giving me a chance when my future was unsure. I played alongside Charles Barkley, who became a lifelong friend, and I had one of the best years of my career. If it were not for that decision, I wouldn't have met my wife and had my amazing son as well as play with one of the best teams in the NBA.

We can empower people so many different ways. We've all heard of successful people who have reached all their goals, and got to the point where their only mission in life was to empower others, to give back. And they gave back to their communities, their families, and their causes.

Why is it so important to empower? Empowering others is the only way you can be completely fulfilled and sustain success. It's also the only way you can transfer power and the gift of the knowledge and success you've learned to others so those qualities can live and breathe on their own.

Every mentor has been mentored; that's a direct reflection of why empowerment is so important. All great leaders have been inspired by books, family, influential people, coaches, and even organizations. To empower people, you must have been empowered yourself.

A few years ago, as I was having dramatic success in real estate, the economy crashed, which devastated the world psychologically and financially. It created a huge opportunity for the thief within to take over.

It affected me and so many around me; it seemed the sky was falling. We were losing real estate, banks were shutting down, and we felt so out of control. I had a sense of anxiety, the first time in my life

I had felt that way. No matter what I did, no matter how hard I tried, everything was collapsing. We were losing left and right, and so was the rest of the world.

One day, I was in the supermarket. I just had to get out of my house. I literally had been in my home for more than a week straight, and I could feel depression setting in. *I have to shake this*, I told myself.

I went to the supermarket to buy the only thing that could cheer me up, a Frost Gatorade. Well, I really love Frost Gatorade. I was standing in front of the Gatorade display when I went into a daze that lasted three minutes or so. I could feel negativity wrapping around my shoulders; I could sense that I was starting to consider giving up. For the first time in my life, I started to think I was failing. I was surrounded by devastation and felt I had no way out.

As I dropped deeper and deeper into this feeling, I suddenly heard a little voice. Well, really, it was an adult voice, but one I remembered as a child. It said, "Mr. Courtney, Mr. Courtney, I like what I see."

My head lifted. My body started tingling. I taught my young basketball camp attendees that phrase to empower them and instill integrity in them. In that split second, my emotions changed. I had tears in my eyes. I turned around and saw a young lady, all grown up, who had been seven when she attended one of my basketball camps.

"Mr. Courtney, it's so good to see you," she said. "I wanted to thank you so much for helping me believe in myself. When you coached me and told me to look in the mirror, look in my own eyes because they do not lie and ask myself, 'Do I like what I see?' and then you said, 'If you don't like what you see, with all your might, go out that day and try to change it because you can control the outcome of your life.'" She repeated the statement I had taught her years earlier.

I couldn't believe what I was hearing. From the depths of the darkness, a seed I had planted years before to empower someone else had come back to actually help me. From that moment on, I took the words I had taught someone else and I applied to them to my own life. I went home, looked in the mirror, and asked myself, "Do I like what I see?" Of course I didn't feel 100 percent that split second, but I knew my direction had changed; my experience had been the catalyst for my resurrection, my comeback, all because of the seed I had planted years before in empowering someone else.

## Pay It Forward

Empowering entails giving someone the authority or power to do something. People relate to this in different ways. If you think of the synonyms—*authorize, entitle, permit, allow, sanction, commission, delegate, qualify, enable, equip*—they all represent forward movement. Empowerment is truly a catalyst for success.

Why empower others? First of all, it gives them permission to be successful. If you think this is a very on-the-edge statement, think about it. So many people are wandering around wanting to be successful. They've read success books and watched success videos. They've dreamed about it; they've thought about it. They've done everything except become successful.

When they finally get a mentor who turns on something inside them, the experience increases their self-esteem and self-worth and gives them permission to become successful.

As you recall in chapter 5, "Expose the Thief," the heart and soul of this book, when you empower others, that starts overwriting negative things that have happened to them. You start to inject a positive influence into their lives, their memory banks, their way of thinking.

When I was younger, I had a lot of negative influences around me. I had a family structure that was very diverse and dynamic, both positive and negative. On one hand, I had been told I couldn't achieve certain things, that I wouldn't amount to anything. That traumatic, devastating experience created my thief within.

But on the other hand, my mother told me, "You can be anything you want to be and accomplish anything you want." That inspired me to start creating the blueprint for my success. I didn't know it at that time, but that little voice became something I held on to when I started accomplishing and achieving things. It became louder every time I pushed myself out of my comfort zone; it finally became the only voice I heard. "I can be what I want to be. I can achieve what I want to achieve. I can do what I set my mind to do."

Through her words, my mother empowered me, and that empowerment effected true change in my life. It's the reason I've achieved things and learned the importance of empowering others. It can start a transformation process in other people's lives; it can give them permission to become successes.

## You Can Accomplish More Together

If you want to change a situation, you have to do something. But if you want to change a community in a positive way, your actions alone are not enough. But I believe that the commitment of one person can change a thousand lives, especially if that commitment is for positive change. By empowering others, you can create that change; empowerment starts the process.

You've probably heard of the butterfly effect. A concept created by Edward Lorenz, it's the idea that a butterfly flapping its wings in one location can dramatically change the weather patterns in a completely different location far away, even contributing to tornados over a long-enough period. If you consider the possibility of a butterfly having that ultimate effect, you can see that each individual effort matters.

You may think that you're insignificant, that what you think or do doesn't matter, but when you commit, when you use these success principles, when you expose the thief and take action, your efforts will have a far greater impact than you realize. You—the sum of your dreams and goals and actions—really matter.

This is why so many people who figure out the secrets of success get to points in their lives where they start giving back and changing things on a global basis. Their individual efforts are not enough by themselves, but when they transfer their knowledge to others, when they empower others, they have a much greater chance of effecting true change.

If you're trying to move boulders by yourself, you can move only so many a day. But if you empower ten other people to move them, you'll move many more as a team. If you could move one hundred boulders an hour yourself and your team members can move only fifty, your team would move five hundred boulders an hour even without you.

This is the reason great players thank their teams in the business world, the sports world, or anywhere else. Extreme achievers win big because they empower their teams. That's why many of them say, "I'd like to thank my team because without them I would never have accomplished all this. We won together." This is the ultimate win; not only do great players or achievers accomplish great things, they do way more as a member of a group than they could have as individuals.

This is true also in life. Planting seeds of positivity and empowerment will bear fruit for years to come. I heard many negative things as a child, but I remember best those few people who planted positive seeds and empowered me as a young man. Now, as an adult, I'm coaching, mentoring, and speaking to other people.

## Empower Family and Friends

Aim at empowering three types of people in your life. Begin with your loved ones—your family and friends. When you empower them, you're empowering your home team. That empowerment will help you and your home team win, and those seeds will bear fruit and spread beyond your loved ones.

Think of empowering your children as they're growing up so they can accomplish great things. The seeds you planted by empowering them will create a legacy for you and your family that will last through the ages. More important, you've given their lives a positive direction, and they will in turn empower and inspire others.

## Empower Your Coworkers

Empowering your colleagues will impact your financial well-being and engender self-worth for you and everyone around you. When you empower your peers and your coworkers, they will go on to help the team win. Empowerment creates a positive work environment in that it can increase production, improve chemistry between workers, and create a successful environment that becomes organic; each project will be characterized by positivity.

## Empower the Leaders of Tomorrow

Developing new leaders through empowerment is by far the best way to lead. It's the key to building a high-performance team, and it allows you to leverage all your assets. Your goal is to develop tomorrow's leaders, not just today's followers. True missions need additional leaders who can carry on the original culture and concept of a work, an organization, a team.

Not every organization operates on this principle. Some structures are based on dictatorship, but the most successful organizations are based on empowerment. These organizations are successful for decades, not just a few years. Leaders who empower through influence live long, happy, successful leadership lives, and they exit gracefully as they watch the culture they created form a new legacy and move on long past their exits.

Dictators, on the other hand, generally have violent and negative exits from whatever they're trying to lead. If you look at the history of dictators—political or corporate—they ended up overthrown by their own people or competitors and generally met violent endings. Dictatorship leads by force; with that type of mentality, you don't allow the natural transition and transformation of leadership of different types, cultures, and religions coming together for one cause.

When you lead through empowerment, you have people from all walks of life who come together for a common cause and create massively great things because they were empowered to do so. The voices they hear are the voices of empowerment that will stay with them their entire lives.

## Ways to Empower Others

### *Encourage Them*

When you encourage others, you're not trying to provide the perfect answer or the perfect situation. Many times, you're just providing them with the platform to air their thoughts and concerns. They will often come to positive conclusions on their own, and you can just back them up with encouragement.

## Give Them Positive Reinforcement

Congratulating others' large and small victories helps keep dreamers on the path to success. Congratulating those who have made an effort to achieve a goal but fell short will make them feel better and will give them permission to try again. Some great successes were born out of failures.

## Listen to Them

Just listening as others express their thoughts can be a powerful way of empowering them because many people never get a chance to be heard. Just by listening, you can make them feel important and feel that their thoughts are actually valid notions.

Try this simple exercise with someone close to you. Explain that this is only an exercise for a study on communication and human behavior so you don't end up hurting anyone's feelings. Get a friend, partner, or family member to tell you something exciting about their lives or something they want to achieve. The first time you listen to them, be totally interested, really engaged in what they're saying; nod your head and show obvious excitement at what they are saying.

Next, have them repeat the same information, but this time, avoid eye contact; start doing something else—maybe text messaging or watching television—let them think you're not paying attention. They will start off as they did the first time, pretty excited, but once they realize you're not paying attention to them, their attitude will become less excited; they may even stop talking.

This is all because people want to believe what they're saying is important. To empower them, make them feel that what they're saying is gold to you. They'll be positive and excited about it, and they'll get more excited about their ideas.

In this age of technology, many of us have lost the ability to communicate properly. We could solve a bunch of the problems we have today if we learned the importance of being truly interested in what others tell us.

## Say Thank You

Thanking others makes them feel valuable and gives them the incentive to do more. If you're leading a group or an organization, you will definitely value this result.

## Create a Framework for Success

As a leader, you must lead, but if you're too strong or lead only by force, you won't give room for your team members to evolve.

Many potentially great leaders have yet to evolve because they've never received the opportunity to do so. Think of how many people you know who are working respectable eight-to-five jobs and making modest livings but not using their talents to the fullest.

So many musicians can play their instruments way better than I could ever dream of doing. I always ask myself, *Why don't they go after their dreams? Why don't they take their talents and actually put the effort behind it and monetize it?* The answers are simple. They don't think their talents are worth anything to anyone else.

My neighbor, a sales exec for a technology company, works hard at an extremely stressful job just like most people in middle management. He also loves music and has a passion for rock 'n' roll. When I visit him, we eventually end up in his music room where he has guitars he plays whenever he finds time. At first, I thought his guitars were just a pastime, a hobby. When I listened to him strum an oldie, I was pleasantly surprised—he was pretty good. When, however, he started to play free-form, from his soul, I heard something amazing, awesome. He was phenomenal when he played from his soul. He almost went into a trance.

I was hearing real talent, amazing music. I said, "That was incredible!" He was surprised and said thanks, but he insisted he was just messing around. Whenever I visited, I would ask him to play from the heart, and each time, I was more amazed. This guy had talent.

I asked him if he had ever thought of creating a CD to share his music with others. He looked puzzled. "Joe, you don't understand," he said. "No one would want to hear this. I'm not at the level of musicians who sell." I knew right away his thief was hard at work. I couldn't sit back knowing what I knew and let my friend miss the opportunity to have freedom through his passion. I asked him to play and record some pieces so I could listen to them, and I eventually got him to do that. I listened. It was beautiful, and I told him so. I suggested he create another CD. He once again compared his music to some greats and knocked his own playing as not being that good. I told him that before every great song became a hit, someone had to hear it. I said that before you worry about what value others might put on your music, let them at least hear it, and do this for your own sake.

He began to play and record. To keep him from comparing his music to others' music, I asked him to think of a word with emotion, such as *love, war, happiness, peace*, and so on, and just play what he felt that word should sound like. This would allow him to focus on just him and the music. I knew that if nothing was shaping people's expectations when they heard it, they would own the music and connect with their own history and have individual experiences with what they heard.

The project began to take flight; each recording was unique and organic. He began to be fulfilled and not hold back while creating balance and an outlet for his stress. My neighbor is happier than ever, and I'm fulfilled for having empowered him to follow his passion. He's now playing for restaurants and private parties and has written his own music.

Through empowerment, positive reinforcement, and encouragement, you can similarly help others leverage their talents and change their lives in the process. Give someone the gift of his or her life. So many of us have suppressed our passions because we don't think our gifts have value to others. Our passions are in us for a reason; they are pressure releases that let us vent and become fulfilled at the same time. Without that pressure release, stress builds and can blow. People can change others' lives with their talents; they will start that butterfly effect by empowering and encouraging others to follow their dreams. This is the whole reason I've written this book. For years, I thought I was alone in the positive and negative experiences I went through. But over time, as I moved from one industry to the next, I realized a common denominator not only in me but also in all people; it just took on different looks, different faces. As I repeatedly saw this, I realized I needed to give myself permission to be successful again and to share with the world. What I have to say and what I feel may be of value to others, and it might just unlock a hidden gem inside them.

The empowerment I received allowed me to empower other people; that came around just in time to help me save my life. It changed me forever, and it was the catalyst for my doing what I'm doing today.

On your journey to success, as you apply the principles in this book to your daily life and start achieving one goal after another, remember to plant those seeds of empowerment because you never know when they might come back to empower you.

The thief within will always exist; its voice, however, will be only as loud as you allow it to be. Through positive reinforcement, you can overwrite that voice with your accomplishments. Through empowerment, you will give yourself and the world a better chance to keep that thief quiet as can be.

Wouldn't it be great if everyone was positive and empowered? But to start this process, you don't change the world first. You don't change the country first. You don't change your region first. You don't change your state first. You don't even change your community or friends or family first. You start with you.

Once you expose and confront the thief, you can start empowering yourself and others. Together, we can empower our community, state, region, nation, country—and eventually the whole world.

No matter what your dream is, my ten success principles will create positive change in you and lead you to success. Applying my principles will give you a bundle of happiness; you'll be 100 percent convinced you can live your life above and beyond the rim.

## Final Preparation before You Take Flight

The ten principles in this book have changed my life. They are designed to first help you achieve personal success and go above your rim to accomplish whatever it is you've always desired. Then through empowering others you can go beyond the rim to reach ultimate fulfillment. These principles have caused me to go above and beyond my wildest dreams and achieve success. I burst into laughter while writing this and shared with my wife that it was amazing how well the principles work. In writing this book, I uncovered my limits, improved on them, and climbed to new heights while reviewing and applying these principles.

When you empower others, you begin reaching the true pinnacle of success in life. The fulfillment you get from changing lives is even better than the fulfillment you receive by increasing your personal performance. For the past few years, I have been leading and coaching people using these principles, and their success and happiness proved to me that this message needed to be shared, so I wrote this book.

You are part of my ultimate success in life. I believe in you; I know God put you here for a purpose, and my mission with this book is to help you realize and uncover that purpose. You were born for greatness; you deserve to be who you were meant to be. The fire burning in your soul is there for a reason; it's time to ignite your passions so they burn brightly for the world to see.

It's time for you to take action! Use these ten principles as a guide to keep you on track so you reach the success you desire. Let's summarize and understand your next move. Start with principles 1 and 2— reconnect with your true desires, and declare and make the choice to really live your life to the fullest to expose your fire within.

Principles 3 and 4 will properly prepare you for your journey by helping you set correct expectations and identify the boundaries of your comfort zone so you won't settle for less than what you are truly capable of.

Principle 5 will be your instant game changer! You will truly expose the thief within and the reason you have been holding yourself back from achieving success.

Principles 6, 7, and 8 will put you on the correct path by helping you create a proper game plan for your success journey. You will also begin the transformation to your new life and have the necessary tools that will hold you accountable to help ensure your success.

Principle 9 will get you off the couch, out of the stands as a spectator watching your life go by, and onto the court, where you'll start playing the game on your terms.

CHAPTER TEN

Principle 10 will help you complete your mission and legacy by teaching you the importance of empowering others to achieve their personal successes. This will truly change your life; it will fulfill you and grant you true happiness and success.

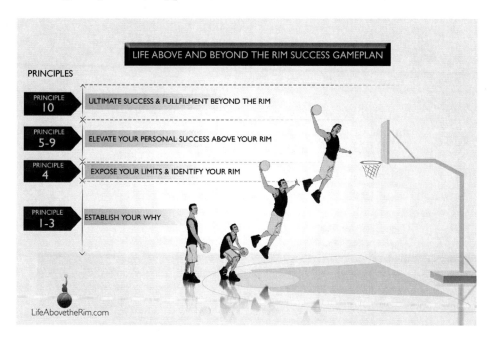

## *LAR SUCCESS GAMEPLAN*

Start your new journey today! Don't wait till it's comfortable; your life is calling you now, so pick up the phone. Become the brilliant, amazing, unique creation you know you are. The world needs you to be the best you can; it's starving for your success. Now is the time to believe in yourself and fulfill your destiny.

We all have unique journeys that will lead to our individual destinies. All the ups and downs we've experienced have been preparing us for this moment, and I'm here to help us all unleash it! We are powerful, we are great, and now we have the tools to prove it.

Live your life above and beyond the rim!

## Exercise Drills to Empower Others

 Make a list of all who mean a lot to you who work hard and have great attitudes and talents but don't believe in themselves. Include anyone you believe in.

 Write them notes or give them calls to let them know how much they mean to you. Say something positive about them, or mention actions they have taken that have made a difference.

 Give them a book or self-help material that can empower their lives. This book is an excellent choice.

 Mentor others by using the principles in this book. Identify their dreams, help them define and declare their choices and directions in life, and assist them in writing a plan. Share their visions with them weekly to help keep them accountable, and assist them with the remaining principles when needed.

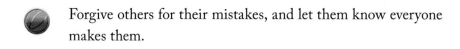

Forgive others for their mistakes, and let them know everyone makes them.

Empower them to grow and lead by influence, not by dictatorship.

Empower them to take total responsibility for their lives.

Give someone a chance if you're in a position to do so.

Share your passion with others; pass on the knowledge that helped you become successful.

# REFERENCES

**Recommended Links:**

Chapter 1
onlinelibrary.wiley.com/doi/10.1002/j.2162-6057.1987.tb00479.x/
abstract) toknowinfo.hubpages.com/hub/Success-Stories-Never-Too-
Old-Never-Too-Late-Late-

Bloomers-Dreams-and-Achievements

healing.about.com/od/visualization/a/powerofmind.htm

psycnet.apa.org/index.cfm?fa=buy.optiontobuy&id=1998-10511-016

www.jstor.org/discover/10.2307/3592833?uid=3739552&uid=
2&uid=4&uid=3739256&sid=21102927082641

voices.yahoo.com/reasons-people-stop-chasing-their-dreams-4609729.html

Chapter 2
www.sciencemag.org/content/311/5763/1005.short

gladwell.com/outliers

www.incomediary.com/how-to-be-like-mike-20-life-lessons-from-
michael-jordan

Chapter 3
money.cnn.com/magazines/fortune/fortune_archive/2006/10/30/8391794/

Chapter 5
www.sciencedirect.com/science/article/pii/S0005796710001324

www.tandfonline.com/doi/abs/10.1080/08870441003763246#.UoKmtfnueSo

link.springer.com/article/10.1007/BF01178214

link.springer.com/article/10.1007/s10608-007-9147-9

link.springer.com/chapter/10.1007/978-1-4614-3661-4_12

link.http://www.erhardseminarstraining.com

link.http://www.recreateyourlife.com

A.D.A.M. Medical Encyclopedia, "Obesity."

www.ncbi.nlm.nih.gov/pubmedhealth/PMH0004552 (accessed May 12, 2012).

Maia Szalavitz. "How Childhood Trauma Can Cause Adult Obesity." content.time.com/time/health/article/0,8599,1951240,00.html (accessed January 5, 2010).

Marcia Stanton. "How Early Experiences Impact Your Emotional and Physical Health as an Adult" (2011). www.pbs.org/thisemotionallife/blogs/how-early-experiences-impact-your-emotional-and-physical-health-adult

Chapter 6
www.historyplace.com/worldhistory/topten/

www.forbes.com/sites/susankalla/2012/05/31/six-keys-to
-excellence-at-anything/

www.leadershipnow.com/leadingblog/2013/06/phil_jacksons
_11_principles_of.html

www.google.com/ url?sa=t&rct=j&q=&esrc=s&source=web&cd=
3&cad=rja&ved=0 CEIQtwIwAg&url=http%3A%2F%2F
www. ted.com%2Ftalks%2Fderek_sivers_keep_your_goals_to_
yourself.html&ei=Rc6AUv2dAaWIyAHOuoHIAg&usg=
AFQjCNFlyJ2IpVWjQ4DufmRPo405aG6zeA&sig2=Cl9cUi65ff
VvFe11sABsiw&bvm=bv.56146854,d.aWc

Chapter 7
www.fhwa.dot.gov/policy/2010cpr/execsum.htm#c1

www.facethefactsusa.org/facts/the-asphalts-getting-crowded-video-
#sthash.KFTzNocE.dpuf

## Recommended Books

The Bible (*NIV*)

Hill, Napoleon. *Think and Grow Rich*. New York: Penguin, 2005. Original edition, 1937.

Lanning, Michael Lee, Lt. Col. *The Battle 100*. Naperville, IL: Sourcebooks, 2003.

Maxwell, John C. *15 Invaluable Laws of Growth*. New York: Penguin, 1937. Updated 2005.

Maxwell, John C. *Developing the Leaders Around You*. Nashville, TN: Thomas Nelson, 1995.

Robbins, Anthony. *Awaken the Giant Within*. New York: Free Press/ Simon & Schuster, 2003. Originally published: New York: Summit Books, 1991.

Singer, Blair. *Little Voice Mastery*. New York: Selectbooks, 2011.

Lefkoe, Morty. "Re-Create Your Life: Transforming Yourself and

Your World with the Decision Maker Process". Kansas City: Andrews McMeel Pub 1977 (Universal Press Syndicate Company) (June 1997)

## *Mentioned Mentors and Coaches*

Tim Grover: <u>www.attackathletics.com</u>
Mack Newton: <u>www.macknewton.com</u>
Phil Jackson: <u>http://www.nba.com/coachfile/phil_jackson/</u>
Jerry Colangelo: <u>http://www.usab.com/bios/colangelo_jerry.html</u>

## *Mentioned Teammates and Inspirations*

Michael Jordan
Charles Barkley
Clarence Weatherspoon
Eddie Johnson
Brett Favre

For more information about Joe Courtney or to
book speaking engagements please go to:
Lifeabovetherim.com
Or
Email: Info@LifeAbovetheRim.com

Book Orders can be directed to:
Joecourtneysbook.com
Or
Contact: 1-855- 5THE RIM

Edwards Brothers Malloy
Thorofare, NJ  USA
January 12, 2015